A Treasury of Woodcarving Designs from Around the World

Alan Bridgewater and Gill Bridgewater

Dover Publications, Inc.
Mineola, New York

Acknowledgments

We would like to thank those people who let us take photographs. A special thanks must go to Peter and John, of BRIDGEWATER and GRAIN, for their help and guidance. We would like to thank the staff of Loughborough Technical College and College of Art Library for their help with research. Finally a big thanks must go to Mrs. E. M. Bridgewater and Mrs. G. Williamson for their financial help.

Credits

Crown Copyright: Victoria & Albert Museum, London
  p. 49 (1); p. 64 (1,3); p. 72 (1,2,3); p. 82 (1,3,4); p. 83 (1); p. 84 (1); p. 85 (1,2,3); p. 93 (3); p. 104 (1,2,3); p. 117 (1,2,3,4); p. 118 (2,3); p. 119 (1,3); p. 132 (1,2,3); p. 133 (1,2); p. 142 (1,2); p. 147 (1,2,3); p. 148 (1); p. 150 (3,4); p. 184 (3,5); p. 186 (2,3); p. 187 (1).

Courtesy: Horniman Museum, Forest Hill, London
  p. 29 (1); p. 33 (1,2); p. 44 (1,2); p. 49 (2); p. 54 (1,2); p. 55 (1,2,3); p. 60 (1,2,3); p. 84 (2); p. 94 (1); p. 101 (1,2); p. 104 (4); p. 165 (1,2); p. 172 (1,2).

Photographs in Authors' Collection, from
Quenby Hall, Leicestershire, England: p. 64 (4); p. 93 (1,4); p. 118 (1); p. 151 (1,2,3,4).
Nottingham Castle Museum, Nottinghamshire, England: p. 29 (2); p. 37 (1,2,3); p. 60 (4); p. 94 (2); p. 150 (1).
St. Mary Magdalene Church, Newark on Trent, Nottinghamshire, England: p. 178 (1,2,3,4); p. 186 (4).
Lincoln Cathedral, Lincolnshire, England: p. 184 (1).
St. Mary the Virgin Church, Bottesford, Leicestershire, England: p. 93 (2); p. 184 (4).
Rutland Museum, Leicestershire, England: p. 64 (2); p. 82 (2); p. 119 (2); p. 150 (2); p. 184 (2).
Belton House, Lincolnshire, England: p. 148 (2,3); p. 187 (2,3).
Alan and Gill Bridgewater: p. 83 (2); p. 186 (1).

Published in Canada by General Publishing Company, Ltd., 30 Lesmill Road, Don Mills, Toronto, Ontario.

Published in the United Kingdom by Constable and Company, Ltd., 3 The Lanchesters, 162–164 Fulham Palace Road, London W6 9ER.

Bibliographical Note

This Dover edition, first published in 1999, is an unabridged republication of the work originally published by Van Nostrand Reinhold Company, New York, in 1981 under the title *A Treasury of Woodcarving Designs*.

Library of Congress Cataloging-in-Publication Data

Bridgewater, Alan.
    [Treasury of woodcarving designs]
    A treasury of woodcarving designs from around the world / Alan Bridgewater and Gill Bridgewater.
            p.   cm.
    Originally published: Treasury of woodcarving designs. New York : Van Nostrand Reinhold Co., c1981.
    Includes index.
    ISBN 0-486-40480-3 (pbk.)
    1. Wood-carving. 2. Decoration and ornament. I. Bridgewater, Gill. II. Title.
TT199.7.B753   1999
738'.4—dc21   98-51586
                                                                  CIP

Manufactured in the United States of America
Dover Publications, Inc., 31 East 2nd Street, Mineola, N.Y. 11501

Contents

Preface

This book is primarily a pattern source manual that draws its inspiration from worldwide woodcarving designs. For those who are searching for vigorous culture-related pattern and ornamentation, this book is essential and indispensable. For those artist/craftspeople whose main concern is woodcarving, we hope this book will become a constant inspirational companion.

We have collected over a thousand carved designs and motifs from sources the world over, including North and Central America, Britain, Europe, Russia, Near East, China, Tibet, Far East, Africa, Iran, India, Oceania, Indonesia, Australasia, and others. For the sake of clarity, we have organized the designs into basic pattern-related groups, so that you will be able to go straight to the section in the book that deals with the type of pattern structures with which you are most concerned. If, for example, you are looking for circle-based pattern, then the "flip" symbols will enable you to turn directly to that specific area in the book. Within each chapter the designs are arranged in groups that have similar historical and cultural roots.

Since the very beginnings of man's development, even the most basic cultures have had a driving urge to produce objects that not only were functional but gave aesthetic pleasure. In many ethnic and tribal instances the role of woodcarving relates more to magic and spirits than to utilitarian objects. The very existence of wood-carved decoration is proof that there is in humankind some inner need for patterns and design. In primitive societies the marks made by the wood-carver are an essential means of cultural communication; the patterns and motifs are symbols that have relevance and meaning within the tribe. When in the late nineteenth and early twentieth centuries European painters such as de Vlaminck and Matisse saw African and Oceanian sculptures for the first time, they labeled them *primitive,* and although we now consider the label to be rather insulting and ethnocentric, it is nonetheless accepted today. Primitive carving tends to be a means of group expression so that the design and shapes can rarely be considered as uncomplicated and unrelated decoration.

In Western societies the carver of wood was usually a person of little social importance. There are, of course, exceptions, one of the most notable being Grinling Gibbons, who, in the seventeenth century, revolutionized English grand house interiors. Also in Western societies the main function of carving was simply to decorate and to please the eye. The exceptions to this were the religious statuary and altar pieces that were the Church's chief means of communicating with a mainly illiterate congregation.

1. Austral Islands—cup; shallow, incised, knife-worked patterns (nineteenth century).

2. New Guinea—weapon motif for knife; cut in shallow relief (nineteenth century).

3. North America (Tsimshian)—stylized eye motif; cut with small adze (nineteenth century).

1

2

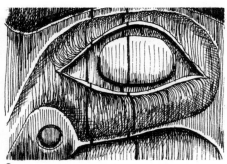

3

Wood is a unique material that can be found in almost every part of the world. It follows that for the student of design, wood-carved patterns must be one of the best primary reference sources. Although there are by necessity a limited number of basic patterns, designs, and motifs, there are many thousands of variations on the simple themes. It is these variations that characterize the style as geographical or cultural grouping.

Western Woodcarving

The culture and arts of the West have passed through many well-defined periods of growth: Romanesque, Medieval, Gothic, and Renaissance among others. Each of these stages is interrelated, however, and so could not have existed or developed in isolation. As the many branches of Western art share the same Graeco-Roman roots, it follows that to a great extent the styles and design motifs have much in common. We now see that the unifying effects of Western Christianity so influenced the direction of the arts that after the Renaissance and the surge of communication that followed, little remained to distinguish seventeenth-century French carving from, say, English work of the same period.

Before the Renaissance in the early fourteenth to the mid-sixteenth centuries, Europe was tribal: The lack of communications meant that art, and especially woodcarving, developed in a direction that depended wholly upon local demand, tradition, materials, and technology. This isolationism resulted in work that was organic in style and rich in individual expression. With the Renaissance, however, Western carving on the whole sought to imitate and repeat nature. This led to the garish and shallow architectural style characterized by an abundance of florid and naturalistically carved flowers, leaves, fruit, and cherubs. This fashion for naturalistic and representational repetition meant that the wood-carvers of the eighteenth and nineteenth centuries became the mass producers of the new age. This desire for slavish repeats led also to the development of molded plaster work and eventually to the demise of the carver. Western carving of the eighteenth and nineteenth centuries gradually became increasingly stereotyped so that anything less than the so-called High Renaissance style, a period of artistic harmony and balance, was considered uncultured and hardly worthy of mention by nineteenth-century aesthetics. By the end of the nineteenth century the art of woodcarving had almost totally disappeared in the West and it was only in certain isolated communities that peasant and folk carving continued to flourish.

Primitive Carving

By the end of the eighteenth century the West had discovered new and exciting regions such as Africa, South America, and Oceania, but as the arts of these societies were outside known and understood art and design thinking, they were labeled "primitive" in a derogatory sense. Until the twentieth century, in fact, primitive carving was considered to be no more than interesting and odd. By the 1920s, however, Western artists gradually began to appreciate the inherent qualities of primitive, primarily African, art.

1. Congo River Area (Basongye)—dance mask; "cubist" lines, adze and knife work (nineteenth century).

2. Norway (Viking)—dragon head from the Oseberg ship; axe-, adze-, and knife-carved (pre-950 A.D.).

3. England, Dorset, Christchurch—prior's stall; adze and gouge work (sixteenth century).

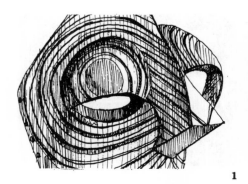

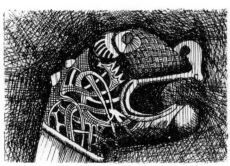

1

2

3

Carved objects are to modern Western eyes aesthetically desirable pieces of art, whereas primitive carvings are considered by their makers to be functional and ceremonial. Primitive carvers are historically "free" in the sense that they are not restricted by recorded traditions that stretch back over many centuries; they refer only to the traditions of the preceding generation. Primitive carvers respond to immediate conditions of geography and technology. The carvers of the Northwest coast of North America, for example, had trade links with Europe, so that they were able to work the tall cedar trees of the area with imported steel tools; the Australian aborigines, out of contact with the outside world and living in largely nonwooded areas, were restricted to scratching small pieces of wood with sharp stones. Although in both these instances tools and available materials are largely responsible for the overall scale of the primitive carving, it is the social conditions that are responsible for the variations of shape, pattern motifs, and function.

In some primitive societies, however, the carvers themselves are part of a complicated ceremonial and ritual structure. The very act of carving is part of a larger and more complex system of tribal and group restrictions; the carving, as far as the carver is concerned, is often an impersonal product of the tribe's religious and social life. An example of this impersonal attitude toward woodcarving was the pre-trade, Northwest coast carvers of the eighteenth century who, according to Captain James Cook's artist, John Webber, "carved the wood. used the carved objects ceremonially, and then left them where they fell."

The amazing variety of primitive wood-carved patterns, forms, and designs is always related directly to three main factors: availability of suitable materials (straight-grained workable woods), availability of cutting tools (bone, stone, or metal chisels and adzes) and a tribal or group need for ritual and domestic objects (religious statuary, ceremonial objects, weapons, food containers, etc.).

In the Introduction we have concentrated our efforts on what could be called primary woodcarving areas. So, for example, we write about Africa south of the Sahara rather than about Islamic North Africa, because we feel that although Islamic decorative traditions—metal working, pottery, woven textiles—are without comparison, the woodworking traditions are related more to wood turning and composite flat work than to woodcarving. In the same way we have concentrated on three main periods of European woodcarving: Viking, Medieval, and Renaissance. Of course Baroque and Victorian work are valid, but in our opinion the complexities of techniques, materials, and mechanization of these later periods are so far removed from the earlier, almost European, tribal traditions, that they are outside our terms of reference. Although the text concentrates on selected main areas and periods, the illustrations are broad-based and are truly worldwide in their coverage.

1. Germany—medieval domestic cupboard; chisel and gouge work (sixteenth century).

2. England, Leicestershire, Quenby Hall—bed; shallow relief gouge work (sixteenth century).

3. England—gilded pine wall bracket; chisel and gouge work (eighteenth century).

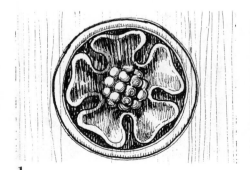

1

2

3

Introduction

For a real understanding of the carved patterns, designs, and motifs, it is necessary to have a closer look at individual periods, cultures, and societies. In the following pages tribal groups, societies, and historical periods are examined briefly, and, wherever possible, motifs, designs, and pattern expressions are explained within the context of their society and environment.

Carving of the Viking and Scandinavian Tradition

During the three-hundred-year period that started about A.D. 800 the Viking influence spread across Western Europe. The mainly Christian chroniclers of the period described the pagan Vikings as pirates, robbers, and Antichrist priest murderers. Of course some of them were all those, but we now know that their main concern was trade and colonization. The Scandinavians were particularly skilled at woodcarving, boat building, and metal work, and it is a combination of these crafts that made long sea voyages possible. The Vikings "pirated," traded, and colonized vast areas that extended east to Russia and west to North America.

Our knowledge of the Viking period and of the Vikings' particularly strong woodcarving traditions comes from the hundreds of archaeological finds that have been made in great ship burial mounds scattered throughout Europe. It was customary to bury high-born and wealthy Vikings in ships that were equipped and stocked as for a long voyage. All the necessities for a "good life" were placed aboard—chests, sleighs, animals, jewelry, weapons. These earth-preserved ship burials provide much evidence to suggest that the Vikings were accomplished carvers of wood. The characteristic woodcarving of this early Scandinavian period is deep relief work depicting interlaced animal, plant, and monster motifs. The carved patterns were all highly formalized, conforming with the Viking desire for convoluted and intertwined design.

As the paganism of the Vikings gradually gave way to Christianity, so Scandinavian woodcarving motifs changed and adapted. Over a span of about 300 years the aggressive pattern and style of the Viking period was modified and simplified until most of the Christian symbols and motifs had been absorbed.

1. Norway, Setesdal, Hylestad Church—folk tale of Sigurd; gouge-cut in deep relief (twelfth century).

2. Norway, Urnes (Viking)—folk tale of the Yggdrasill beast; gouge-cut in deep relief.

3. Norway—medieval wool box; shallow, gouge-carved motif.

1

2

3

Danish, Swedish, and Norwegian communities continued up until the nineteenth century to have a strong wood technology, and their houses, churches, boats, furniture, and a great many of their domestic artifacts were constructed from large, deeply carved slabs of wood. As the European Renaissance influenced Scandinavia, so the buildings and furniture reflected the change by a new framed and panelled style of construction. This fashion for elegant panelled rooms and furniture made deeply carved surfaces technically unsuitable, but the desire for a profusion of carved pattern lingered on.

As a generalization we think it fair to suppose that the survival of the Scandinavian carving tradition can be attributed to the geography of the region. The deep fjords, the rugged mountain passes, and the harsh climate meant that many rural communities remained isolated well into the nineteenth century. This isolation permitted the woodcarving styles to retain their individualism. While many of the more accessible border areas of southern Denmark and Sweden succumbed and adopted the repetitive ornament of the sixteenth-century Italian High Renaissance style, other more traditional northern rural areas continued to carve in the fourteenth-century medieval and Gothic styles.

The rural farming life-style called for simple and strong furniture, warm wooden room interiors, and a host of small domestic kitchen and dairy ware. When we now refer to Scandinavian woodcarving we have in mind those ordinary domestic items that have their roots in the powerful traditions of the Vikings. Many of the motifs, such as the twined vine and the acanthus, are symbols that were used by Graeco-Roman architects and craftsmen, but the chip-carved, circle-based roundel designs and the twined beasts may be attributed to the Viking pagan style. The carved motifs most characteristic of work that has resisted Romanesque and Renaissance influences are usually based upon twined animal motifs and simple geometric pattern. It is these that could best be described as Scandinavian.

In common with much of Europe, Scandinavia in the nineteenth century saw a period of mass production, experimentation, and new materials. For woodcarving, this meant a deterioration of orthodox techniques and methods. Like other European and Western countries, Norway, Sweden, and Denmark became conscious of the old, the rural, the romantic, and the folk traditions during the late nineteenth and early twentieth centuries. The resulting arts and crafts revival brought about a surge of interest in old patterns, motifs, themes, and working methods. In rural Norway, Sweden, and Denmark today one still finds a healthy woodcarving cottage industry, but it is fast becoming just another tourist and export production. There are still many small isolated communities that use carved items related to their way of life, but, because of television, travel, and increased communications, the carvers are absorbing foreign patterns and mechanized methods, which tend to debase their traditions.

1. Norway—house door post; flat chisel-carved (fourteenth century).

2. Norway—Romanesque chair back; shallow chisel- and knife-cut.

3. Sweden—mangle board; chip-carved (nineteenth century).

1

2

3

English and European Carving

During the first half of the fourteenth century, England and Europe were unifying and emerging from a period of ignorance, social unrest, and cultural instability. This gradual recovery resulted in the development of permanent communities and the construction of large stone buildings. The Church was particularly active in this period of expansion, and everywhere there were signs of renewed artistic and craft endeavor. Since wood, and especially oak, was plentiful, it was used lavishly to panel and decorate church and cathedral interiors. In this climate of artistic richness and social confidence, the artists, architects, and craftsmen extravagantly displayed their skills. Very soon the churches, cathedrals, and large houses were liberally decorated with animal- and plant-related patterns and representational motifs. Everything was carved from wood: linenfold wall panels (carved representations of folded cloth), ceilings, roof beams, doors, benches, tables, altars, and chests. The period initiated the rise and prosperity of carvers and woodworkers. Within all this woodcarving activity, however, there were many religious and social dictates related to representational statuary. These imposed religious design and theme limitations and required that the master carvers work mainly on repetitious patterns and morality themes. At first it was felt that the carvers of wood should copy the patterns and motifs of the stone masons; they even went so far as to paint and texture the wood to imitate stone; but fortunately the versatility of wood as a unique building material triumphed.

As a general rule the master wood-carvers of the medieval period worked with a team of apprentices and one or two finishers or improvers. The master supervised the total design and layout conception, and under his watchful eye the apprentices roughed out the work with small hand adzes and removed the bulk of unwanted wood. The improvers then took the work almost to completion, but the final details and finish were left to the more accomplished and practiced hands of the master. There is some question as to how much of the carving was done by the masters, but it must be supposed that they did the prestigious carvings that were in full view.

In certain areas—beam ends, the undersides of stalls and seats, and misericords (bracketed projections on the undersides of seats in a choir stall, used to afford rest to a standing person)—because of the inaccessibility and relative humbleness of the carving, it is likely that the work was done by very skilled but rather unsophisticated workmen. These skilled carvers worked on themes drawn from their immediate and everyday activities, and so it is that the carvings often illustrate scenes and motifs that are earthy, domestic, romantic, humorous, and sometimes even pornographic. They show games, sports, jokes, bawdy tales, myths, costumes, customs, and a host of details that give us a unique insight into the way life was lived. The pity is that we are almost totally ignorant about the identity of the individual carvers; their names were never recorded and, with one or two exceptions, the carvings remained unsigned. The Victorian Romantics of the middle and late nine-

1. France—canopy stalls; chisel and gouge work (fifteenth century).

2. England—church bench end "poppy" or terminal; three-dimensional chisel and gouge work (fifteenth century).

3. France—naturalistic border design; gouge work (fifteenth century).

1

2

3

teenth century who drew their inspiration from the medieval period saw the carvers as free-thinking, vital, expressive artists who had an overwhelming urge to create new and exciting forms. The facts of the matter are more simple and direct—the carvers, working for wages, either illustrated their own experiences or borrowed designs and themes from manuscripts, books, and woodcuts.

By the late seventeenth century the original power of the medieval style of carving was so weakened and overworked that the strength of the designs was lost. Over the centuries prudes and religious bigots have destroyed the more base carvings, followers of new fashions and styles have altered many works, and unappreciative vicars, priests, and church wardens have modernized church interiors, so comparatively few examples of medieval church carvings remain.

Because Renaissance is the label placed upon an indefinite period of development that links the Middle Ages with modern times, there are no precise dates that mark the beginning, the middle, and the end. For our purposes, however, it can be taken that the "new beginning" started in Italy some time in the fourteenth century and during the fifteenth and sixteenth centuries influenced France, Spain, and the rest of Europe. It was a period when the attitudes and intellectual activities of Europe responded to a revival of interest in ancient learning. The progressive climate of adventure, communications, and artistic striving culminated in the discovery of new lands and the expansion of social, political, and intellectual awareness.

The "rebirth" involved the total structure of society, but we have, for reasons of clarity, limited this section almost entirely to furniture, which we think best demonstrates the effects of the Renaissance on the style of woodcarving. Of course the great churches, cathedrals, and grand houses boasted magnificent altar pieces, screens, and revolutionary architectural structures, but for the most part these were made of stone and precious metals.

Obviously the Renaissance was a time of tremendous growth in all the arts, but for the wood-carver it was primarily a period when new techniques of furniture making made the old deeply carved designs and motifs unworkable. New and expensive exotic woods were being imported from the Indies and used to make delicate, portable, framed, and panelled furniture. These conditions brought about a shift of emphasis away from the massive, gouge-cut work of the thirteenth century and toward shallow decorative pattern and applied surface methods of decoration such as inlay and marquetry. The direct and naive approach of the Medieval woodworkers gave way to excessive and exaggerated detail.

Some authorities think of the Renaissance as a period of elegance and refined proportion; others consider it a period when artists and craftsmen became faddish copyists. Whatever the attitude, it was certainly an age when craftsmen revived old traditions, invented new working methods, and experimented with new materials. The wood-carvers worked in a style that related closely to classical Greek and Roman architectural works. The carvers' main opportunity for expression was in the popular desire of the rich for delicate, elegant, exotic furniture. Of all the many furniture-decorating techniques that developed during the Renaissance, inlay, marquetry, and other methods of applying thin sheets of exotic woods to wood surfaces was the one that related best to the classical devices that characterized the

1. England, Dorset, Christchurch—elbow on choir stalls; deep, undercut gouge work (late fifteenth century).

2. France, Rouen, St. Etienne des Tonneliers—misericord; undercut chisel and gouge work (fifteenth century).

3. England—oak chest; chip-carved motif (fifteenth century).

1

2

3

11

popular pattern themes. The furniture designs relied on the use of architectural pattern repetition, with the consequent abundance of carved colonnades, inlay friezes, and pierced facades. Linked with this departure from the austere forms of earlier periods was a greater understanding of joinery and furniture-building techniques. Furniture was no longer massive and restricted to benches, tables, and chests. The woodworkers experimented with panelled and framed cupboards, tables, beds, and chairs, all of which emphasized comfort and style over functional durability.

It was not until the early fifteenth century that the Renaissance influence made itself felt in England; even then it was partially held back by the very powerful, orthodox linenfold style of carving that was still popular there. Traditionally English woodworkers had favored oak, and this preference for a coarse and difficult-to-work material resulted in the chunky, functional English Renaissance style. This style declared itself best in the furniture that was popular during the reign of James I (1566–1625), the period now referred to as Jacobean. The design elements that were the most common feature of the furniture of the English Renaissance were the plum-shaped turned legs of tables and cupboards and the flat relief strap-work (ornamentation in the form of interlacing bands) on panels and furniture.

The spirit of the Renaissance prospered until the beginning of the seventeenth century; it was then gradually replaced by a period of architectural illusion, painted ceilings, and luxurious materials which we now refer to as Baroque. Although the Baroque style of woodcarving has some validity as far as technique, method, and decoration are concerned, it is also a period when European woodcarving traditions became decadent and debased. To generalize, it could be said that the Baroque style was the catalysis on the force that began the decline of European woodcarving. It was certainly a period when wood-carvers became mechanics rather than artists.

1. England—mirror frame motif; chisel- and gouge-carved (mid-eighteenth century).

2. England—panel carved by Grinling Gibbons for Cosimo III, Duke of Tuscany (Cosimo Panel); worked with chisel, gouge, and knife, built-up (seventeenth century).

3. England—gilded candle stand motif; gouge-worked in pine (eighteenth century).

Folk Woodcarving—The Balkans

The four countries that make up the Balkans are Albania, Bulgaria, Romania, and Yugoslavia. Although under communist rule the Balkans are gradually becoming industrialized, the region continues by geographical necessity to be divided into many small, isolated, rural communities. The Balkan folk arts bear witness to long years of Turkish, Greek, Austrian, and Russian colonization, but the crafts, especially woodcarving, continue to be relatively unspoiled and inspired.

The woodcarving of the peasants reflects the early traditions of the Roman and the Byzantine Empires; many of the motifs — the classical eagle and the Christian cross, for example—are still being used, albeit in barely recognizable abstraction. Woodcarving in the Balkans is mainly the craft of the men. Shepherds and peasant farmers pass the time chip carving small personal and domestic objects for themselves, their wives, their sweethearts, or their children. Cups, spoons, boxes, picture frames, saltcellars, nutcrackers, and butter stamps are among the most common. The main tool used for the carving was, and still is, the small hand or clasp knife; the technique is nearly always shallow geometrical chip carving. The wood is worked green, that is to say, in an unseasoned moist condition. The surface to be carved is colored red, blue, or black, and the designs are cut through the colored coat to the wood beneath. This method results in crisp and sharp-edged designs. Usually the carver cuts and assembles the article before the carving begins. Many elements, especially the spoon and cup handles, are carved in the form of birds and flowers, others are cut with crests and initials. Finally the carved objects are patterned with crosses and zigzags, the spaces in between being filled with triangular chip-cut patterns.

Many Balkan houses and cottages are built and decorated by the villagers themselves. The gates, beams, walls, pillars, rails, doors, and furniture are all heavily decorated with shallow notch-cut or chip-carved patterns, living examples of peasant art. Conditions are changing rapidly, but in the early part of this century it was quite common for village churches and large community buildings to be constructed by group effort. The peasant villagers carved the beams and benches with powerful (and at times bizarre) motifs and patterns, such as coiled snakes and severed heads. The church, with its heavy carved doors and exterior pillars, usually has a carved and gilded tower. Around the church are dozens of tall, roofed, and heavily carved crosses, a gate, and a fence—everything is carved.

The village farmyards are fenced, and entrance may be gained through massive post-and-lintel gateways. To protect the farm from evil spirits, the gate posts are carved with serpents, Christian motifs, such as the cross, and masses of geometric pattern. Often this gateway is topped with a wood shingle roof and the whole structure is patterned with woodcarving and traditional decorative iron work. These gates can be found in many Balkan states, but they are most typical in central Romania.

1. Romania, Suceava—domestic chest; very shallow, incised design (nineteenth century).

2. Austria, Salzburg—mangle board made in the village of Lungau; shallow knife and chisel design (nineteenth century).

3. Romania—distaff; pierced and incised (nineteenth century).

1

2

3

Images from Africa

At the beginning of the nineteenth century, Africa, as far as the West was concerned, was a land of the unknown and the "primitive." The masks and cult figures. that gathered dust in museums and private collections were wondered at for their bizarre qualities, but were intellectually and artistically ignored. At the beginning of the twentieth century certain young artists of the "anti-classical" school "discovered" African masks and fetish figures (idols supposed to possess supernatural powers) and began to create art works that were extensions of the African styles. Artists such as Picasso and Matisse began to use motifs, images, and styles that were essentially African. By about the middle thirties, the work of these artists was admired and universally accepted; as an offshoot of this interest, scholars such as Roger Fry and Franz Boas declared African sculptures to be "works of art."

It must be realized, however, that although to early twentieth-century artists African sculptures were in a sense "modern," they are in fact objects that are related to tribal and social traditions many hundreds of years old. Although it is only logical to suppose that woodcarving was done in earlier periods, rapid breakdown due to a humid atmosphere, termites, and wood rot is responsible for the lack of pre-eighteenth-century work.

Africa is divided geographically by the Sahara desert, which stretches in an east-west direction across the continent. North of the Sahara, the people have been so influenced by Muslims and Middle Eastern culture that their wood sculpture cannot be thought of as purely indigenous. (Although Islamic decorative traditions are superlative, because of the scarcity of timber a high value has always been placed on even the smallest fragment of wood. It is for this reason that Islamic wood-worked articles are composite and so generally speaking fall outside our terms of woodcarving reference.) In this discussion, "Africa" means the vast area south of the Sahara. Isolated and protected by forests and mountain barriers, the people of this area have developed woodcarving traditions that are unique.

To understand a little of what African carving is about, it is necessary to have some knowledge of the social structures that governed the lives of the people. Basically, African traditional societies were feudal, in that the individual tribal members obeyed the family elder, who in turn looked to the village headman, who in his turn looked for leadership to the tribal kings and chiefs. For the majority of African tribal societies, this system usually resulted in communities that were stable and so were able to develop a settled subsistence agriculture and skills such as pottery, carving, and weaving. These relatively secure tribal groups were able to further establish and evolve complex political, religious, and artistic customs. The tribes drew the basic essentials of life from the immediate environment—mud, wood, and grass for shelter; animal hides and vegetable fibers for clothing; meat, milk, and maize for food; clay for pottery; and soft and hard woods for tools, weapons, bowls, furniture, masks, and cult figures. Of all the crafts, woodcarving, because of its many practical applications, was perhaps the most vital. The tools

1. Africa (Ibo)—crested dance mask; pierced and knife-worked (mid-nineteenth century).

2. Africa—society mask; adze- and knife-worked, the striated patterns painted (nineteenth century).

3. Mali (Bambara)—Chi Wara dance mask motif; relief-carved (nineteenth century).

1

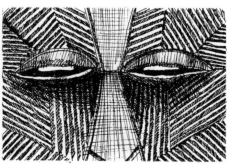
2

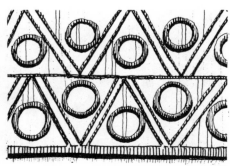
3

used were either made locally or obtained through trade; these included the adze, the curved knife, and the bow drill.

In an environment where transport was difficult and written communications limited, traditional methods and skills were passed on by word of mouth and by direct observation. Also, because examples of carved work deteriorated within a couple of generations, there were few examples of old work for the carvers to imitate. This resulted in styles, motifs, and methods that always referred to the immediate past.

Obviously, the shape of the final carved form can also be attributed to the variety of wood used, the tools, and the intended function of the carving, so if we are trying to learn more about the motifs and patterns, we must look at specific tribal regions. Primarily woodcarving falls into three categories: that carved for use in the home—bowls, dishes, headrests; that carved by professionals and related to status—staffs, headrings; and the special cult religious and ritual objects that were needed for the ceremonies—drums, stools, statuary. In almost all African carving the patterns, motifs, and images function either to placate spirits or to represent family and ancestral spirits and gods. This is not to say that some of the carved motifs and patterns were not used purely decoratively. The carver often worked in isolation, perhaps in a sacred glade or hut; his aim was to create a sculpture that could be entered by the spirits and to this end he used special tools, performed the appropriate ceremonies, and made sacrifices. In all instances, although the methods and motifs were subject to gradual change, the overall concepts were based on long-established precedents.

Ghana—Ashanti

The Ashanti have very few woodcarving traditions and are known primarily for their gold casting and their strip cloth weaving. They do, however, carve curious pulley wheels for their loom heddles. The Ashanti weavers think of the carved figures as "watchers" who care for and guard the cloth as it passes through the loom. They also carve ceremonial stools and fertility dolls; these dolls, which can be recognized by their discoid heads, were carried by girls to increase fertility and promote beauty.

Guinea—Baga

The Baga people, who live on the coast of Guinea, carve many masks and figures that personify the fertility of the tribe, animals, and crops. At the time of the rice harvest a huge head and breast figure with chip-carved patterns is carried shoulder-high around the village. This *nimba* or fertility motif is also carved on other ceremonial items and it is thought that the ripe curves of the face and the breasts are intended as physical channels through which the spirits of fertility can be communicated. Nimbas are usually carved in a heavy hard wood, the surface of which is patterned with chevrons and lines intended to represent complex hair coiffures and tribal markings. Since the tribes in this region mark their skins with decorative scarring, it is probable that many of the carved patterns are thus inspired.

1. Ivory Coast (Baule)—mask; adze- and knife-carved (nineteenth century).

2. Congo River Area—music clapper motif; knife-carved in shallow relief (nineteenth century?).

3. Ivory Coast (Dan)—dance mask; adze-carved in the round and then highly polished (nineteenth century).

1

2

3

Ivory Coast — Baule

It has been said that the carvings of the Baoule are the most "aesthetic" and popular to Western eyes. Perhaps this is because we can sympathize with their naturalistic, almost Western, ideas of realistic interpretation. In the nineteenth century the Colonial French who governed the Ivory Coast admired the Baoule carvers to the extent that they encouraged them to make carvings for export. This commercialization weakened the style and resulted in a poor, rootless repetition of form and design. As well as carving ancestral figures, fetish sculptures, and masks, the Baoule make a variety of domestic items—heddle pulleys for looms, stools, ceremonial canes, rods, and whisks. The Baoule masks are characterized by slit and bulging and plum-shaped eyes, smooth surfaces, and "carved hair" patterns.

Mali — Bambara

The Bambara tribe is organized around agriculture, animal husbandry, and ancestor worship, so they tend to place an emphasis on fertility, tribal care, and ancestor protection in their religious carved sculptural masks. The masks are typified by the long-horned deer and antelope styles—many of the animal forms are so abstract that the original subject is hardly recognizable. The masks are worn during the harvest dance dramas, when the dancers parade through the fields and villages. The masks are horned, abstract, and composite, and they are finely chip-carved with furrowed lines, chevrons, and geometric patterns.

Nigeria — Ekoi

It was the naturalistic, skin-covered, carved heads of the Ekoi tribe that first inspired Roger Fry, the London art critic of the 1920s to declare, "This is art indeed." The carved, life-like heads, with their horns and deer skin covering, are worn by the tribe elders at funerary dances and cult meetings. When early nineteenth century explorers first observed the masks and heads, they thought they were looking at preserved human heads. This tribe and the neighboring Ibibio also carve impressive masks and helmets. Often made in honor of a chief, they are representational in that they have eyes, nostrils, and cheeks, but are often covered in regular furrowed patterns, which tend to weirdly abstract the basic form.

Mali — Dogon

Although the Dogon have traded with their Muslim neighbors, they are physically and culturally isolated. This insularity has resulted in a woodcarving style that is unique. The carved work of the Dogon is, with the exception of the young men's masks, made by the smith, and consequently is heavily influenced by blacksmithing tradition. In Dogon society the blacksmith is a man apart: He is a worker in metal and a carver of wood, but primarily he is a magician and a link with the spirit world. The blacksmith is responsible for carving all the ceremonial masks and ancestor figures. These figures are carved for the specific purpose of housing the spirits of the dead, and, once they have been made, they are kept in caves and secret places and brought out only on special ceremonial occasions. The carvings, whether they be figures or masks, are carved in deep relief and in a style that is vertical, lean, ascetic, and architectural. Elongated carved figures of the first Dogon ancestors sit together in erect primordial contemplation; the bodies of the figures are often carved with crisscrossed lines and chip-carved triangular motifs.

Gabon — Fang

The carvings of the Fang tribe are divided roughly into two groups; the dance masks, which are usually heart-shaped and painted white, and the figures that guard the reliquaries containing ancestors' bones and relics. The purpose of the reliquary figures was to protect the ancestors from evil and to signify that the area around the bones was taboo. Often the designs of carved furrows and ovoids are seen clearly, but sometimes the pattern is obliterated by an oily black patina, probably chicken or goat blood.

Congo — Basongye

The carvings of this tribe, who are also called Songe, are characterized by lines that follow the carved form; the main curves of the form are exaggerated by carving furrows over the whole of the carved surface, and the masks usually have slit bulging eyes. The lines are filled with colored pigments and various resin gums. The features of these "cubist," striated masks are so abstract that the underlying design subject is barely recognizable.

Congo — Bayaka

This tribe uses carved fetishes, from which it considers that it gains its power. Even more easily identified than the fetishes, however, are the carved, painted, and raffia-applied "young men's masks." Although these are usually carved by the village carver, they are painted and decorated by the young men themselves. Bayaka masks and heads are characterized by a flattened, upturned nose and painted chalk white features. Although vast numbers of these masks have been made for the tourist trade, they are well carved and are difficult to distinguish from earlier nineteenth-century examples.

Congo — Bena Lula

Carvers of great skill, this tribe makes small gnome-like figures characterized by spiral weals and patterns on the joints, buttocks, and faces. They are usually burnished and patinated with oil and resin. Because many of these figures are carried around and so have to be portable, they are rarely more than one foot high. These guardian or protection figures are supposed to watch over property and to guard their owner.

In all African carving, the patterns, designs, and motifs are so interdependent with function and societal context that they cannot be considered in isolation as art forms. In a great number of instances twentieth-century communications and colonialization have destroyed the cultural meaning of the woodcarvings; if wood is still carved it is usually in support of tourist commercialism. This is not to say that all modern African carving is without artistic significance—if it is done well it has validity.

The Heraldic Crest Carvers—Native Americans of the Northwest Coast

Of all the areas in the world where woodcarving has been practiced, the Northwest coast of North America has, by modern artistic standards, produced some of the most stimulating, colorful, and exciting work. The work of the Tlingit, Tsimshian, Haida, Kwakiutl, and Salish people who lived on this coast is of special interest to the student of wood-carved design.

The traditional homeland, which runs from Yakutat in Alaska, south to the Columbia River in Oregon, of these tribes is flanked by the Pacific Ocean to the west and vast forests to the east. These vast forests were rich in straight-grained cedar and birch trees, and from these two very workable woods the people obtained bark for textiles and canoes, timber for houses, and wood for all manner of domestic ware. The craft of woodcarving became the major occupation of the various tribes. Their woodworkers made boats, boxes, houses, "hot stone" cooking vessels, weapons, totem poles, household objects, and masks, hats and other personal ornaments. Within these societies, prestige and social position were achieved by possessing as many richly carved and painted craft objects as possible.

Although the carving methods and motifs of the different tribes are similar, it is the extent to which the carvings are painted and the colors used that characterizes the different tribal styles. To generalize, the carvings of the northern tribes are relatively plain, using perhaps two earth colors, whereas in the south, the carvings are painted with as many colors as can be obtained.

The tribes claimed links with the people from their myths and supernatural tales to the extent that they themselves actually changed their names and took on the personalities of the animal beings who "lived" in the legends and stories. This change of identity necessitated the carving of masks, large heraldic totem poles, and symbolistic dance and drama regalia. Ceremonial feasts were part of the ritual and it was during these feasts that tribal nobles established their rights by giving bowls, boxes, and masks carved with their heraldic insignia. Totem poles, which are the most obvious symbols of rank, were displays of heraldic insignia that recorded episodes in the spiritual and temporal life of an individual or his ancestors. Many of the carved symbols and motifs recorded actual heroic events, while others were records of supernatural events.

Although there is archaelogical evidence to suggest that the Native Americans of the Northwest coast have, from earliest periods, carved, it is thought by anthropologists that the woodcarving of large totems has been possible only since the eighteenth and nineteenth centuries when European steel tools were introduced by fur trappers and traders. The principal tools used by the Tlingit, Tsimshian, Haida, Kwakiutl, Nootka, and Salish carvers were the steel gouge, adze, and knife. The

1. North America (Tsimshian)—chief's chest; carved in shallow relief and painted (nineteenth century).

2. North America (Haida)—totem pole; three-dimensionally surface-carved with knife and adze and painted (nineteenth century).

3. North America (Tlingit)—wooden plaque; carved in shallow relief with knife and adze and painted (nineteenth century).

1

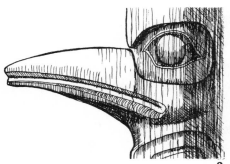

2

3

carvers and workers of wood understood joining, steam bending, laminating, pattern making, and three-dimensional carving; using these techniques and those relatively simple tools, they made everything from the walls of their houses to plates and canoes.

Since nearly all the elements of the carved design were related to myths, legends, and clan lineages and had to be interpreted by all tribe members, it was important that the various carved characters and motifs be boldly conventionalized. The carvers developed a method of dividing up the various views of the subject and carving all on the same plane. So it is that the top view, back view, and profile of the figure carved are all seen as a single flat, stylized, almost diagramatic design. Gradually, over many generations, this almost child-like, cubist system of symbol and animalistic motifs developed, so that carvings could be interpreted or "read" by all tribe members. The carvers were able to shift the emphasis of the carving by concentrating on individual design elements, so that a front view of eyes, nostrils, and claw gave one story variation while the profile with a single nostril gave another. The overall design impression that the carving gives is of framed circles, eyes, and ovoids. Designs on flat surfaces were most subject to this formal and abstract graphic approach, so that carvings of this type are most frequently found on the sides of chests and the walls of buildings. Many of the objects that had to be carved in the round because of their function—a bowl or ladle for example—were carved in a manner that was both graphic and three-dimensionally naturalistic. For example, a frog-shaped bowl might be carved realistically to represent a frog but stylized abstract patterns and motifs would be carved on its flat surfaces. When the carvings were complete the surfaces were tooled and textured. At a later stage the various elements of the carved design were painted, outlined, and emphasized with flat primary colors.

Unlike many ethnic carving traditions, the work of the Northwest coast Native Americans has continued well into the twentieth century; with the growth of interest in the arts there has been a renewal of interest in carving from this area. Because artists and craftsmen of the west also have a heraldic and decorative woodcarving tradition, they find it relatively easy to identify with the carving methods and designs of these people; perhaps the craft will continue to develop and flourish.

1. North America (Haida)—bear rattle; knife-carved, painted, and built-up (eighteenth to nineteenth centuries).

2. North America (Haida)—animal-headed bowl; three-dimensionally adze- and knife-carved, then surface-carved and painted (nineteenth century).

3. North America (Tlingit)—stylized bear face motif; knife- and adze-carved and painted (nineteenth century).

1

2

3

The Enigma of the Ainu Wood-Carvers—Japan

The Ainu number 15,000 to 16,000 and of these now only about 400 are full-blooded; the remainder are an Ainu-Japanese mix. At an earlier period they may have occupied both islands of Japan but they are now scattered over only small areas of Hokkaido, Japan's northern island. They are a short, muscular people who differ physically from their Japanese neighbors in their fair skins, large, round, dark brown eyes, and black wavy hair. Because of the last physical characteristic they are called "Hairy Ainu" by their Japanese neighbors. It is believed by some that the Ainu are a remnant of a Caucasoid people who originated in northern Asia; others believe that they are from Mongolian-Chinese stock; and another school of thought believes them to be a race apart. Whatever is true, we know that as a result of centuries of Japanese and Chinese migration, many of the Ainu traditions have been lost. Although it is almost certain that within a few more generations the Ainu will be completely overwhelmed culturally by the Japanese, this people still manage to retain many individual religious beliefs and distinctive cultural traditions.

As with many other rural, isolated, ethnic communities, for the Ainu handicrafts are vital to their way of life. In their rather closed society, the tasks of day-to-day living are classified as being masculine and feminine: The women manage the house and work with fabric, embroidery, weaving, and leather, while the men traditionally hunt and carve wood, bone, and horn. Carving is considered an essential masculine accomplishment. Men carve bows, arrows, swords, scabbards, and household utensils, and boys are trained in the use of special knives and advised as to the suitability of wood types.

As with most of the other crafts, the patterns, designs, and motifs of the Ainu are to a great extent directly related to materials, tools, techniques, and function. The Ainu carver works with a knife, uses a close, straight-grained wood, and carves from nature. These craft limitations result in delicate, shallow relief animal and plant motifs. Very little is known about pre-nineteenth century Ainu carving, but from old Chinese and European prints and accounts we are almost certain that the most important techniques, methods, and designs have survived. Today many of the distinctive Ainu motifs and patterns have been swallowed up by Japanese traditions and styles, but a few characteristic designs remain relatively untouched.

The rituals of Ainu culture and religion require very specific ceremonial spoons and knives carved with characteristic spiral and scroll motifs. The customs that relate to puberty and marriage are complicated, but as we understand it, girls approaching puberty are tattooed around the mouth with a special carved knife, an indication that they are marriageable. When the girl finds a husband, he customarily gives her a special knife sheath that he himself has carved. These are just two examples of the many instances when carved instruments were, and sometimes still are, used or given ceremonially.

1. China—furniture motif; pierced and built-up (eighteenth century).

2. China—wardrobe cupboard toe or plinth board; shallow raised work (eighteenth century).

3. China—chair back slat motif; gouge-worked in shallow relief (eighteenth century?).

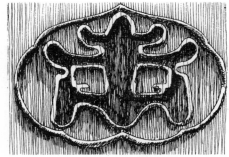

1

2

3

In addition to spirals and scrolls, the main pattern structures are based on circles and hatched lines. Many of the motifs have a structure similar to Chinese peasant carving and it is thought that there may be some distant cultural connection between the two. The ceremonial and ritual objects of the past required that the motifs be symmetrical and related to recognized and accepted design themes. This placed restrictions on personalized carving, but from the endless pattern variations it is obvious that there was room for considerable interpretation.

As the new generation of Ainu attend Japanese schools and colleges, the traditional crafts and customs are being gradually absorbed. It is probable that within another generation the wood-carved designs, motifs, and techniques will be lost and forgotten.

1. Japan (Ainu)—weapon motif; knife-incised (nineteenth century).

2. Japan (Ainu)—knife handle design; shallow knife-incised (nineteenth century).

3. Japan (Ainu)—domestic utensil motif; knife-incised (eighteenth to nineteenth centuries).

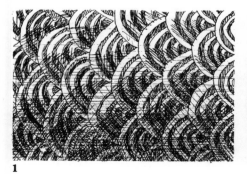

1

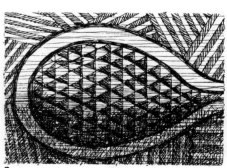

2

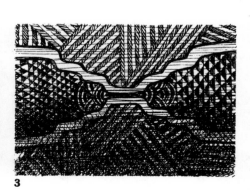

3

Oceania—Spirit and God Carving

Oceania is the name given to the 10,000 islands scattered throughout the South and West Central Pacific Ocean. This vast area, which extends over about one-sixth of the earth's surface, contains a wide variety of craft traditions important for the student of woodcarving and ethnic design. Although the anthropologists divide the Oceanian cultures into six different areas of study—Australia, New Zealand, Southeast Asia, Melanesia, Micronesia, and Polynesia—they are, as far as we are concerned, areas that contain similar woodcarving environments.

Until recently the people of these islands had a relatively stable society that was centered around root and tree cultivation, chicken and pig breeding, and saltwater fishing. Kinship ceremonies, hunting, and organized warfare were major cultural activities, so it was necessary to have complex symbolistic regalia. These vital ritual and cult trappings were made using simple basalt, jade, and shell adzes and knives. Although the environments, tools, and materials of these scattered peoples were similar, the carving styles and the motivations for the carving were not altogether comparable. However, as a very broad generalization, it could be said that the ceremonies were based on spirit and god placation; therefore, most of the woodcarvings are either in the form of decorated ceremonial tools and utensils or spirit, god, and ancestor statuary.

In hot damp climates wooden carvings are subject to all manner of fungus and termite attacks, and it is for this reason that they rarely survive for long periods. The Oceanian carvings that now exist were collected no earlier than the eighteenth and nineteenth centuries, when Europeans first made contact with that part of the world. Modern carvings are, of course, still being collected, but the depth of the patterns and the shape of the motifs are so influenced by the introduction of steel tools, formal education and the media that they cannot be compared with early work.

In the island societies everyday domestic carving was the task reserved for adult males. The designs tended to spring from materials and tool types rather than from conscious "artistic" endeavors. Shallow chip-carved patterns and incised and notched work are the most efficient ways of decorating large surfaces, so designs of this type were the most common. When it was important that the carver have a special knowledge of magic, understand certain tools, or have specific skills, a village carver gifted in the supernatural was employed. In many instances, such as in carving door lintels, decorating canoe prows, or shaping ancestor masks, it was necessary to observe particular taboos and religious rites. The patterns that were carved were nearly always stylized and organized according to long-standing traditions. The masks and religious regalia were carved in a manner that was always linked directly with tribal and cultural memories, so it was only over many generations that unconscious changes in patterns and motifs gradually occurred. With

1. New Caledonia—boar or pig mask; carved in the round, knife and adze work (nineteenth century).

2. New Caledonia—house roof terminal; three-dimensionally-carved with knife and adze (nineteenth century).

3. New Guinea, Lake Sentani—house gable decoration; shallow relief knife work (nineteenth century).

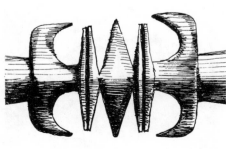

1

2

3

carvings of this character, even the smallest carved marks and motifs were regarded as deeply significant. The carvers, so far as we understand, had no wish to carve in a style that was personal or innovative; indeed, they considered themselves not artists but religious and cultural communicators. This is borne out by comparing documented early eighteenth-century and nineteenth-century carvings, which show virtually identical patterns and motifs, with very little evidence of individual expression.

Many of the carved masks and totems were of significance only as long as a ceremony lasted. They were not considered as valuable art objects, but only as temporary symbols and "homes" for the spirits. After they served their purpose, they were discarded. It was for this reason that early missionaries and collectors were able to gather carvings that had lost their spiritual importance. When in 1774 Captain James Cook visited Tonga, his men picked up "curious carved work" that was scattered along the beaches like so much driftwood.

It is almost impossible to make clear distinctions between the carved pattern and motifs of the various cultures because, in most cases, there are overlappings of religious beliefs, taboos, and traditions; but it is possible to make generalizations about the main cultural carving styles.

New Zealand—Maori

In a climate that is temperate, the Maori lived in large houses and huts, and so a style of woodcarving that was architectural soon developed. The carvings tended to be functional as well as symbolic, and the Maori used a soft, easily worked wood. The carvings are based on naturalistic and animal themes and show spiralled infill pattern work. The carved gable ends usually show full frontal ancestral figures and stylized "bird men," flanked by lesser figures and spiral motifs. The spiral and hanging tongue motif as used in Maori carving is, it is believed, related to much older work that has been found in Southeast China. Recently excavated Taiwanese bronzes have shown a very strong connection between the two cultures.

Melanesia

Melanesia includes New Guinea, Solomon Islands, Santa Cruz, New Hebrides, Loyalty Islands, New Caledonia, and Fiji. Land dwellers and inshore fishermen, the Melanesians carved in many styles and for very many cultural reasons. In New Guinea most of the carved work was functional—adze handles, paddles, canoe prows, house facades, headrests. However, these were also surface-carved with chip-carved patterns of ancestral figures and myth people to protect the owner of the carving. As with most primitive societies, masks also played an important part in the religious life of the New Guineans; they believed that while the dancer wore the mask, he actually became the spirit that the mask represented. The people of New Guinea were organized into secret societies that practiced ancestor and animal cults and to this end they carved masks that became for them physical and earthly extensions of the spirits of the dead. The motifs and patterns are all part of a strictly executed carving tradition. In New Guinea the spirit and ancestor ceremonial shields that hang in the cult houses are functional in that they obviously

1. New Zealand (Maori)—stylized face; three-dimensionally-carved, then surface-patterned with knife and adze (nineteenth century).

2. Marquesas—house post; relief-carved (eighteenth to nineteenth centuries).

3. New Zealand (Maori)—house lintel motif; pierced and chip-carved in shallow relief (eighteenth century).

1

2

3

offer physical protection in battle; but they are also relief-carved with sacred images that are declarations of rank and status. The Melanesian woodcarving forms are recognized by characteristic squatting figures, eye motifs, naturalistic ancestor masks, and virility and fertility figures.

Polynesia

The Polynesians are racially mixed peoples who inhabit the central and eastern islands of Oceania, the major among them Cook Islands, Samoa, Tonga, and Tahiti. The woodcarvings of these peoples are characterized by stylized god figures and beautiful chip-carved ceremonial paddle blades and weapons. The people built large log canoes and traveled from island to island, so the canoe became a central theme in their woodcarving, the paddles became objects of high ceremony, and the carved figures on the canoe prows represented gods. Many of the best carvings of these islands were destroyed or taken by nineteenth-century missionaries, but they are on record as being carved in hard wood and as being smooth, black, and shiny in appearance. The carvings of this area are best characterized by ritual paddles covered in fine chip-carved patterns. The designs consist mainly of parallel and zigzag lines that completely cover the surface. In some areas the delicate patterns are filled with white resin gum mastic and shell inlay; the decorated area is then burnished. This results in a hard polished surface smooth to the touch.

To write exhaustively on all aspects of woodcarving, on all areas, and all periods would take a lifetime, and the result would fill a small library. We have, therefore, limited our terms of reference to what we call "primary wood carving," that is work that is closely related to tools, materials, and techniques, and we concentrate almost exclusively on concepts of carving that are either primitive in the sense of being tribal, or primitive in the sense of being pre-eighteenth-century European.

To offset what some may think of as an imbalance, our illustrations and captions are broad-based and there are examples from most periods and countries. To make meaningful reference, cross-reference, and comparison possible, we have grouped the illustrations according to their structure and form. Each caption describes the tools, techniques, and materials, and the photographs place the designs and motifs in context.

Chapter 1

Lines

African Tribal

1. Congo River Area (Basongye)—mask, detail; knife-carved and painted (nineteenth century).

2. Cameroons (Bacham)—monkey mask, detail; knife-carved (nineteenth century).

3. Ivory Coast (Baule)—dance mask, detail; knife and chisel work (nineteenth century).

4. Ivory Coast (Baule?)—domestic utensil decoration, detail; knife-carved (nineteenth century).

5. Congo River Area—wooden goblet, detail; knife-carved in shallow relief (nineteenth century).

6. Ivory Coast (Senufo)—"human" mask, detail; knife- and chisel-carved (nineteenth century).

7. Mali (Bambara)—crocodile dance mask, detail; knife-carved in shallow relief (nineteenth century).

8. Angola and Congo River Area (Bajokwe)—stylized hair pattern on a statuary figure; knife-carved (nineteenth century).

9. Sierra Leone (Mende)—figure used in ancestor worship, detail; adze- and knife-carved (nineteenth century).

10. Sierra Leone (Mende)—ancestor figure, detail; knife- and chisel-carved (nineteenth century).

28

1

1. Nigeria (Yoruba)—three-dimensional "mother" figure; adze, gouge, and knife work (nineteenth century).

2. Tonga—war club; shallow knife chip carving; this example is included here because, technically, there are many similarities between African and Oceanian carvings (eighteenth to nineteenth centuries).

2

Tribal Triangular

1. Maii (Bambara)—Chi Wara dance headdress, detail; shallow relief knife carving (nineteenth century).

2. Africa (Baluba)—wooden bowl, detail; chip-carved (nineteenth century).

3. Samoa—club handle, detail; chip-carved (nineteenth century).

4. Sierra Leone (Mende)—Bunda society mask, detail; knife chip-carved (nineteenth century).

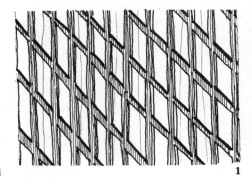

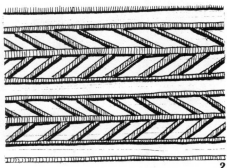

1. Congo River Area (Bambala)—bowl, detail; chip-carved (eighteenth to nineteenth centuries).

2. Ivory Coast (Baule)—drum motif; chip-carved (nineteenth century).

3. Romania, Transylvania—salt cellar; chip-carved and filled with white mastic (nineteenth century).

4. Africa (Baluba)—chief's arrow holder, detail; knife chip-carved (nineteenth century).

5. Cameroons—characteristic pattern, detail (nineteenth century).

Chip-Carved Triangular

1. Mali (Bambara)—Chi Wara antelope mask headpiece, detail; simple knife cuts (nineteenth century).

2. Romania, Transylvania, Cluj—pair of folk-carved nutcrackers, detail; knife-worked chip carving (nineteenth century).

3. Ivory Coast—characteristic drum pattern, detail (nineteenth century).

4. Ivory Coast—drum, detail; very simple and direct chip carving (early nineteenth century).

5. Mali (Bambara)—Chi Wara dance mask, detail; knife-worked line and triangle (mid-nineteenth century).

6. Upper Volta (Mossi)—dance mask, detail; chip-carved, pierced, and painted (late nineteenth century).

7. Mali (Dogon)—man's staff, detail; knife chip-carved and polished (nineteenth century).

8. Romania, Transylvania, Bistritsia—peasant spoon, detail; wood is stained and the chip-carving reveals the white sapwood (nineteenth century).

9. Ivory Coast (Baule)—water container, detail; adze-carved and knife chip-carved (nineteenth century).

10. Congo River Area—pattern from a headrest, detail; simple direct chip carving (nineteenth century).

1

2

1. West Africa—headrest; three-dimensional adze and knife work (eighteenth to nineteenth centuries).

2. New Zealand (Maori)—feather box; shallow chip-carved pattern covers the entire surface of the box; rather more complex than African chip carving (eighteenth to nineteenth centuries).

African and Oceanian Primitive

1. Trobriand Islands—handle of a lime spatula or paint stick, detail; shallow chip-carved design was probably cut with a shell knife (nineteenth century).

2. Admiralty Islands—canoe prow, detail; patterns such as this were carved with simple adzes and knives, and they were sometimes filled with a white mastic or polished shell fragments (eighteenth to nineteenth centuries).

3. Guinea—Simo society mask motif; adze and knife worked (nineteenth century).

4. Santa Cruz Islands—fish motif; probably cut with an iron knife (nineteenth century).

5. Mali (Bambara)—Chi Wara dance headdress, detail; adze and knife work (nineteenth century).

6. Ivory Coast (Guro)—antelope dance mask, detail from the horn pattern; knife-worked and polished (early nineteenth century).

7. Africa?—paddle, detail; knife and adze work (nineteenth century).

8. Africa (Bajokwe)—pattern detail from a strut that braces the legs of a chief's chair; chisel- and gouge-worked to a highly polished finish (nineteenth century).

9. Manus Islands—commemorative dish, pattern detail; chisel- and knife-carved (nineteenth century).

10. Mali (Bambara)—Chi Wara dance mask, detail; worked with adze and knife (nineteenth century).

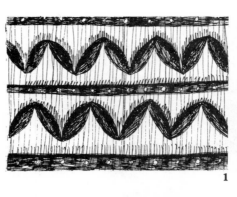

1

2

3

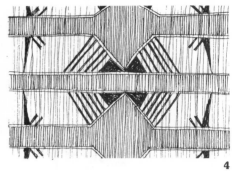

4

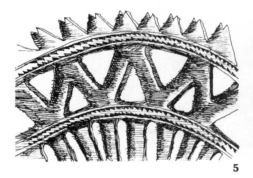

5

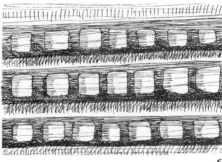

6

7

8

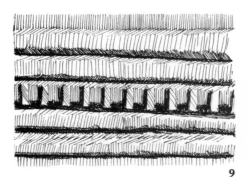

9

10

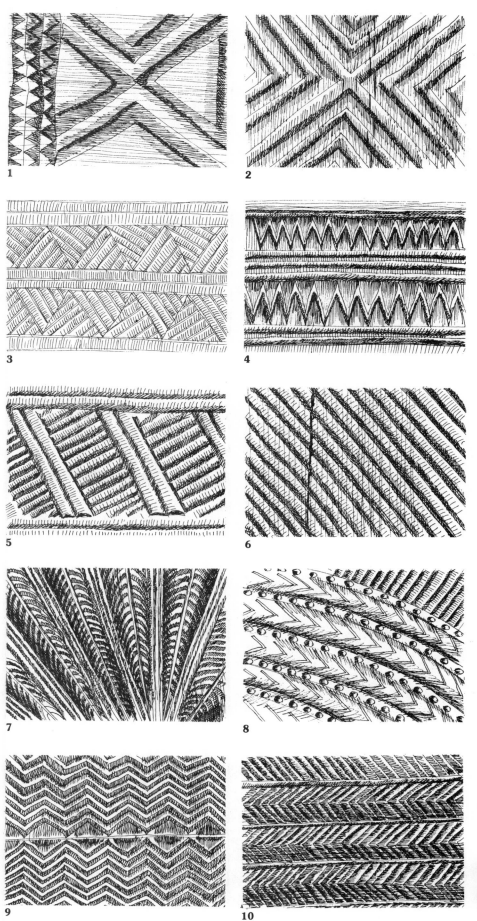

1. Mali (Bobo)—mask, detail; knife-carved and painted (nineteenth century).

2. Congo River Area (Bena Lula)—loin cloth of a fetish figure, detail; adze, gouge, and knife work (nineteenth century).

3. Nigeria—comb, detail of pattern; close-grained hardwood, worked with knife and chisel (nineteenth century).

4. Africa (Benin)—domestic bowl; gouge-carved and worked with a knife (sixteenth to seventeenth centuries).

5. Africa (Bajokwe)—tobacco mortar, detail; worked with adze and knife to a highly polished finish (eighteenth to nineteenth centuries).

6. Nigeria (Yoruba)—stylized hair texture in a three-dimensional sculpture, detail (eighteenth to nineteenth centuries).

7. Nigeria (Yoruba)—head area of a traditional sculpture, detail (eighteenth to nineteenth centuries).

8. Guinea (Baga)—head of a Nimba fertility mask, detail; probably carved with an adze and knife (nineteenth century).

9. Africa (Baboyo)—stylized chest motif from a "man" statue; three-dimensionally-carved with adze and knife (nineteenth century).

10. Guinea (Baga)—head of a drum figure, detail; carved with adze, gouge, and knife (eighteenth to nineteenth centuries).

African Texture

1. Sierra Leone (Mende)—Bunda society mask/helmet, pattern detail; worked with knife and adze (nineteenth century).

2. Dahomey—handle of a royal staff, detail; worked with a knife (nineteenth century).

3. Nigeria (Yoruba)—ancestor image, detail; carved with a knife and adze (eighteenth to nineteenth centuries).

4. Nigeria (Yoruba)—ancestor figure, detail; shallow relief work with knife and chisel (nineteenth century).

5. Gabon—handle of a domestic spoon, detail; probably carved with a knife (nineteenth century).

6. Guinea—comb, detail; knife-carved in a fine, close-grained wood (eighteenth to nineteenth centuries).

7 and **8.** Guinea Coast—mask of the Poro society, detail; worked with adze, gouge, and knife (eighteenth century).

9 and **10.** Congo River Area—tankard; gouge-carved and knife-textured (nineteenth century).

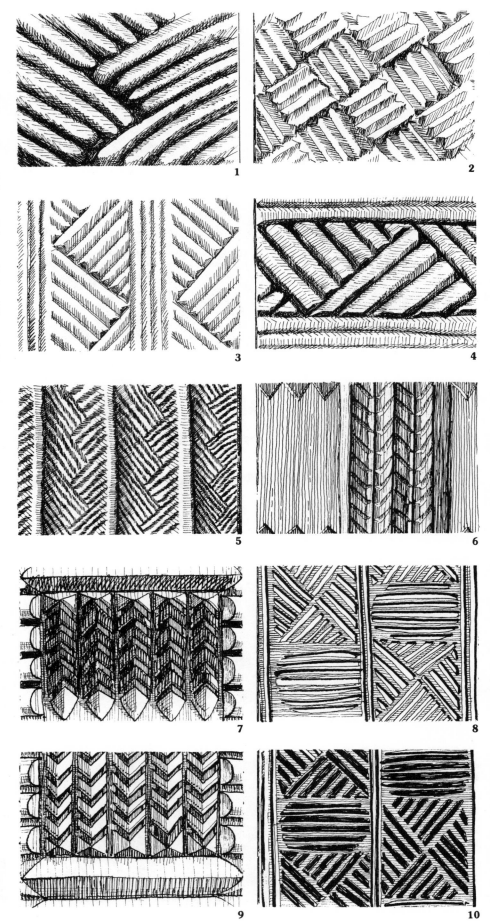

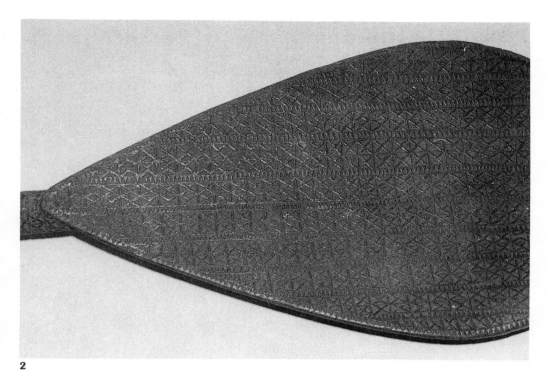

1

2

3

1. Nigeria—comb; knife-carved and incised in very hard wood (eighteenth to nineteenth centuries).

2. Polynesia—paddle; shallow chip carving; the marks made by specific tools are a decisive factor in the formation of pattern structures and, in many ways, this Oceanian carving could be mistaken for African work (eighteenth to nineteenth centuries).

3. Africa—gourd storage container; knife chip-carved and incised pattern (nineteenth century).

Furniture Inlay

1. Spain—cedar and brier wood box; cut and inlaid with an irregular check motif, highly polished (seventeenth century).

2. Spain—motif from a characteristic Spanish Renaissance secrétaire; inlaid with cedar and brier (sixteenth century).

3. Spain—motif from walnut and boxwood inlaid cabinet (sixteenth century).

4. Spain/Portugal—typical inlay design for a cabinet; there is very little attempt to make the cut regular (seventeenth century).

5. Switzerland—Renaissance chest; the pattern is large (the illustration is about half size) and it is an inlay rather than marquetry (sixteenth century).

6. Europe—"Antwerp" table; the inlay is made from wood and shell (seventeenth century).

7. Italy—pattern from the lid of an Italian cassoni, detail; these coffin-shaped chests were often elaborately carved and inlaid (sixteenth century).

8. France—pattern from an "Empire" worktable; the three-wood perspective design is characteristic of the eighteenth and nineteenth centuries (nineteenth century).

9. Spain—chest; common pattern (sixteenth century).

10. Italy—inlay border from a cassoni chest (sixteenth century).

1. Spain/Africa—furniture motif; deep inlay (eighteenth century).

2. England—motif from a nonesuch chest; these large inlaid chests usually featured architectural motifs in the forms of palace buildings in the design (sixteenth century).

3. Spain—motif from a cedar and brier box; the workmanship is typical of the furniture made by the peasant carpenters of rural Spain (seventeenth century).

4. France—Louis XV commode; diamond and floral marquetry design (eighteenth century).

5. England—cabinet; a large, rather rough design made by a rural craftsman (eighteenth century).

6. France—motif from a rolltop desk; three woods are used (eighteenth century).

7. Italy—desk top, detail; very simple optical arrangement (sixteenth century).

8. France—Versailles commode; a three-wood, very precise design, highly polished (eighteenth century).

9. England—sideboard or court cupboard motif (seventeenth century).

10. Italy—cassoni chest motif (sixteenth century).

Oceanian Pattern

1. Solomon Islands, Bougainville—dance shield motif; deep chip carving with knife and adze (nineteenth century).

2. Tonga—war club motifs; very delicate knife chip carving (nineteenth century).

3. Solomon Islands—dance shield pattern; a mastic-filled, knife chip-carved design (nineteenth century).

4. Admiralty Islands—characteristic domestic utensil design; chip-carved (nineteenth century).

5. Solomon Islands, New Georgia—hair pattern from a canoe prow figure, chip-carved (eighteenth to nineteenth centuries).

6. Cook Islands, Mangaia—pattern on a ritual adze; knife-carved, highly carved adzes were carried by tribe elders as a badge of office (nineteenth century).

7. New Ireland—incised pattern from the head of an Uli statue; worked with adze and knife (nineteenth century).

8. Tonga—pattern from a war club; characteristic basket weave design; worked with a knife (nineteenth century).

9. New Ireland—pattern from the breast area of an Uli statue (nineteenth century).

10. Santa Cruz Islands—design from a carved fish; three-dimensionally chip-carved (nineteenth century).

1. Austral Islands—zigzag motif from a war shield; knife-incised (eighteenth to nineteenth centuries).

2. Solomon Islands—dance shield pattern; a very large, boldly carved and painted motif (nineteenth century).

3. Tonga—deep relief pattern from the handle of a war club (nineteenth century).

4. Solomon Islands, Bougainville—dance shield pattern; carved in shallow relief with knife and adze (nineteenth century).

5. New Zealand (Maori)—motif from a chief's feather box; knife-carved (eighteenth to nineteenth centuries).

6. Solomon Islands, Bougainville—pattern from a dance shield; shallow relief carving with adze and knife (nineteenth century).

7. Tonga—characteristic chip-carved pattern; very regular and highly organized grid (nineteenth century).

8. New Caledonia—deep relief pattern from a roof gable apex; adze- and knife-carved (nineteenth century).

9. New Caledonia—house post pattern; adze- and knife-carved (nineteenth century).

10. New Caledonia—door frame motif; deeply carved with adze and axe (nineteenth century).

Squared and Scooped

1. Africa, Ivory Coast—square-cut drum motif (eighteenth to nineteenth centuries).

2. Norway—drinking vessel rim pattern; probably cut with a V-shaped gouge (eighteenth to nineteenth centuries).

3. Africa (Baga)—incised grid pattern; knife-cut (nineteenth century).

4. England—Elizabethan service with shallow relief carving pattern around the rim; chisel and gouge work (sixteenth century).

5. Spain—cupboard door motif; planed and gouged (sixteenth century).

6. Norway—cup motif; worked with chisel and chip-carved; characteristic of north European work (eighteenth to nineteenth centuries).

7. Africa, Ivory Coast—design from the handle of a comb; shallow chip carving (nineteenth century).

8. Sierra Leone (Mende)—motif on a carved figure; probably knife- and adze-carved (eighteenth to nineteenth centuries).

9. Africa, Ivory Coast—domestic bowl design; knife-worked (eighteenth to nineteenth centuries.)

10. New Caledonia—door post decoration; deeply carved, probably with an adze (eighteenth to nineteenth centuries).

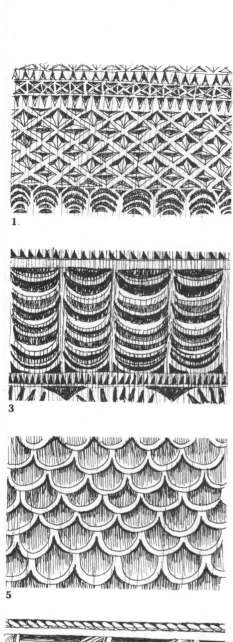

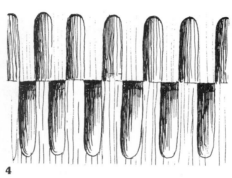

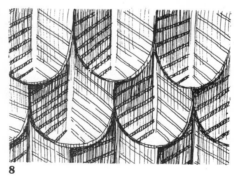

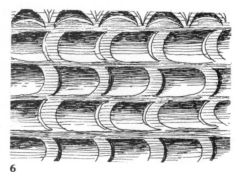

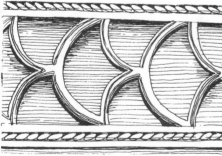

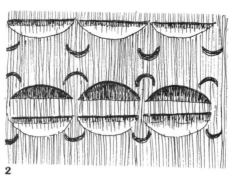

1. Austral Islands—cup; characteristic Oceanian chip-carved decoration, worked with knife and adze (nineteenth century).

2. Switzerland—bed; very simple and direct gouge pattern (seventeenth century).

3. Cook Islands, Mangaia—weapon decoration; chip-carved and deeply gouge-cut (eighteenth to nineteenth centuries).

4. Sweden—frame for holding a watch; simple gouge cuts (nineteenth century).

5. Norway—drinking vessel total coverage pattern; design worked out on a grid of gouge cuts (nineteenth century).

6. Spain, Basque Provinces—pattern on the stretcher (strut that braces the legs) of a chair; gouge-cut (sixteenth to seventeenth centuries).

7. Norway—decoration on a domestic laundry board; chip-carved with a gouge (eighteenth century).

8. Norway—drinking vessel pattern; gouge cuts and knife work (nineteenth century).

9. Netherlands—Dutch chest; shallow relief gouge work (nineteenth century).

10. Spain—chest, very similar to Spanish work of the early eighteenth century; gouge-cut (nineteenth century).

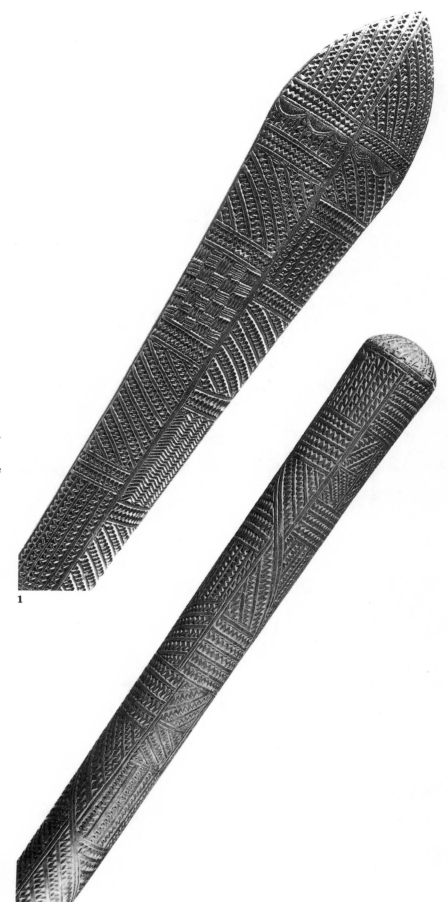

1. Tonga—war club; shallow chip carving (eighteenth century).

2. Tonga—chip-carved club; adze and knife work (nineteenth century).

1

2

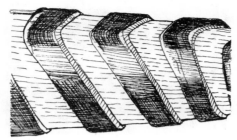

African Pole Carving

1. Congo River Area—club handle; finely carved, probably with a knife (early nineteenth century).

2. Ivory Coast (Guro)—horn from a mask/helmet of the Zamle society; relief-carved, highly polished (early nineteenth century).

3. Ivory Coast (Senufo)—neck area of a three-dimensionally-carved spirit figure (nineteenth century).

4. Congo River Area—baton or staff of state, detail; knife-carved (nineteenth century).

5. Sudan—pattern from the handle of a spoon; knife-carved (eighteenth to nineteenth centuries).

6. Sudan—pattern from the handle of a grain crusher; knife-carved (eighteenth to nineteenth centuries).

7. Africa—horn area of an antelope mask, detail; knife-carved, thick, brown, encrusted patina (nineteenth century).

8. Congo River Area—handle of a mirror, detail; knife-carved (nineteenth century).

9. Congo River Area (Bakwele)—horn from a dance mask; knife-carved (nineteenth century).

10. Loange River Area—deeply carved hatchet handle; worked with knife and adze (nineteenth century).

1

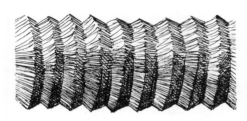

3

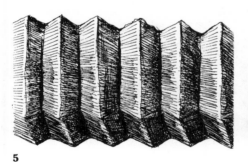

5

7

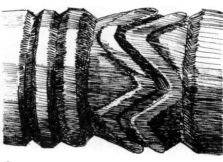

4

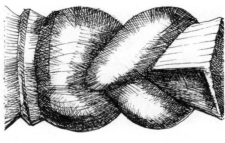

6

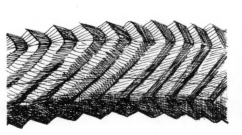

9

10

New Guinea Weapon Decoration

1. New Guinea—adze- and knife-carved shield motif; carved in shallow relief and painted (nineteenth century).

2. New Guinea—dance stick pattern, detail; this particular design was inlaid with a white lime mastic (nineteenth century).

3. New Guinea—shield motif; very large patterns of this character were cut with an adze and then painted (eighteenth to nineteenth centuries).

4. New Guinea—dance pole pattern; very shallow carving, almost scratch pattern, probably worked with a knife (nineteenth century).

5. New Guinea—border design from a shield; a very characteristic, bold motif carved in shallow relief (nineteenth century).

6. New Guinea—spear shaft decoration; this illustration is approximately four times the actual size; knife-carved (nineteenth century).

7. New Guinea—band of pattern from a spear shaft; knife-carved (nineteenth century).

8. New Guinea—dance stick design; finely carved; this illustration is approximately twice the actual size (nineteenth century).

9. New Guinea—border pattern from the top half of a shield; adze- and knife-carved (nineteenth century).

10. New Guinea—weapon border pattern; knife-carved and painted (nineteenth century).

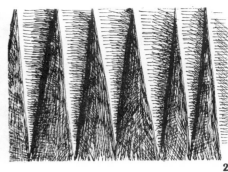

1

2

3

4

5

6

7

8

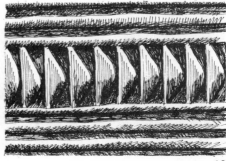

9

10

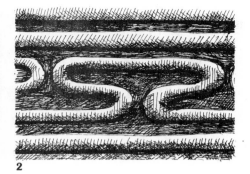

1

2

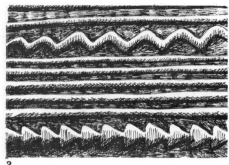

3

4

5

6

7

8

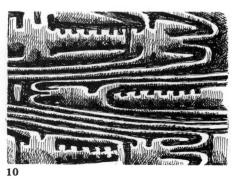

9

10

1. New Guinea—spear shaft pattern; probably carved with a small bone or stone knife (early nineteenth century).

2. New Guinea—dance pole band pattern; carved with a primitive knife and then inlaid with lime mastic (early nineteenth century).

3. New Guinea—domestic container pattern; patterns of this type are usually found around bowl rims and shield borders (early nineteenth century).

4. New Guinea—spear shaft pattern; the structure of this particular design relates to the human figure; probably carved with an iron knife (nineteenth century).

5. New Guinea—dance stick pattern (nineteenth century).

6. New Guinea—shield border motif (nineteenth century).

7. New Guinea—spear shaft design; knife-carved (nineteenth century).

8. New Guinea—most New Guinea wood-carved patterns are simply decorative, but humanistic patterns of this character have a spiritual significance (nineteenth century).

9. New Guinea—very carefully worked dance stick design; incised with a knife (nineteenth century).

10. New Guinea—shield pattern; the early carved pieces were worked with stones, shells, adzes, and knives; and the motifs and patterns were ceremonially and religiously significant (eighteenth to nineteenth centuries).

Hearts and Flowers

1. England—stay, busk, or corset stiffener love token motif; incised pattern carved with a knife (eighteenth century).

2. England—knitting needle sheath motif; incised and chip-carved with a knife in pine (eighteenth century).

3. England—stay, busk, or corset stiffener love token motif; these were about one foot long and usually carved in a light, knot-free pine wood (eighteenth century).

4. Romania, Transylvania—razor case; chip-carved and incised; simple objects such as boxes or handles were carved or whittled by peasants and shepherds (nineteenth century).

5. England—love token motif; knife-carved (eighteenth century).

6. England—love token motif; shallow incised, knife-carved (seventeenth to eighteenth centuries).

7. Norway—butter mold motif, very characteristic of Scandinavian wood-carved patterns of the eighteenth and nineteenth centuries; chip-carved in light and knot-free pine (eighteenth century).

8. Russia—flask built-up and carved by a Crimean soldier as a love token; chip-carved (nineteenth century).

9. Romania, Transylvania—decoration on a door post and lintel; adze, knife, and gouge carving (thirteenth century).

1

1

1. Norway—domestic bowls of this character
were common features in rural households; they
were usually carved from such taste- and smell-
free woods as pear and sycamore (nineteenth to
twentieth centuries).

2. England (Flanders)—ell measuring stick; chip-
carved (nineteenth century).

2

49

Japanese Ainu Incised Patterns

1. Japan (Ainu)—decoration from the sheath of a short sword; chip-carved and incised, worked with a knife (nineteenth century).

2. Japan (Ainu)—sword sheath decoration; incised patterns of this kind typify nineteenth century Ainu carving (nineteenth century).

3. Japan, (Ainu)—sword sheath; although this pattern is Ainu, it is very similar to Japanese and Chinese work of the nineteenth century; incised and chip-carved (nineteenth century).

4. Japan (Ainu)—pipe case motif; chip-carved and incised, knife-worked (nineteenth century).

5. Japan (Ainu)—moustache raiser, used when eating to keep the moustache dry; pierced and gouge-worked; the Ainu carved and decorated combs, pins, and cutters (nineteenth century).

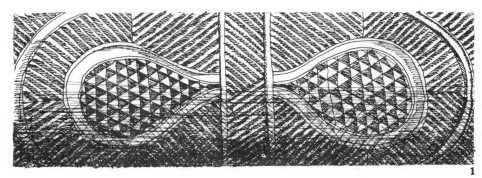

1

2

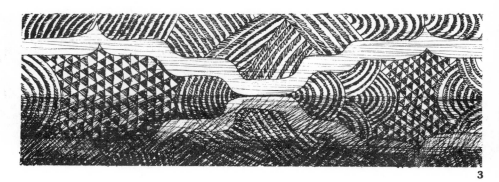

3

4

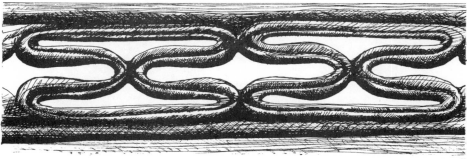

5

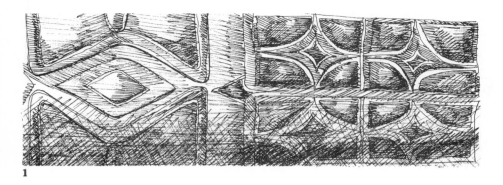

1

2

3

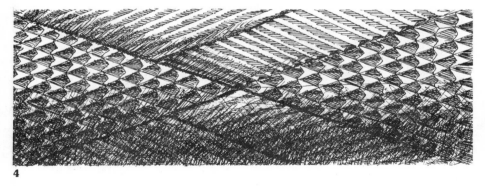

4

5

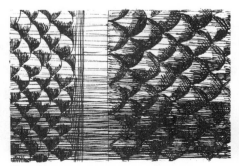

6

1. Japan (Ainu)—quiver design; knife- and chip-carved (late eighteenth century).

2. Japan (Ainu)— ritual spoon decoration; chip-carved and knife-incised (eighteenth to nineteenth centuries).

3. Japan (Ainu)—very characteristic shell motif on a man's hunting knife handle (nineteenth century).

4. Japan (Ainu)—knife handle; chip-carved (nineteenth century).

5 and **6.** Japan—motifs taken from a tobacco container; chip-carved and incised (nineteenth century).

Chinese Furniture

1. China—pierced swastika design on bed/couch rail; built-up and gouge-worked (seventeenth to eighteenth centuries).

2. China—clothes stand motif; pierced and built-up (eighteenth to nineteenth centuries).

3. China—foot stool top; built-up and jointed (nineteenth century).

4. China—bed or couch balustrade; built-up and jointed, worked with traditional Chinese woodworking and carving tools (eighteenth to nineteenth centuries).

5. China—bed/couch balustrade (seventeenth to eighteenth centuries).

6. China—couch arm balustrade (eighteenth to nineteenth centuries).

7. China—pierced end of a side table; one of the main characteristics of Chinese domestic furniture carving of the late eighteenth and nineteenth centuries is the rounded profile of all the main woodwork (nineteenth century).

8. China—pierced design from a small, drum-shaped stool (seventeenth to eighteenth centuries).

9. China—bedstead balustrade, detail (nineteenth century).

10. China—carved leg bracket of a side table (nineteenth century).

1

2

3

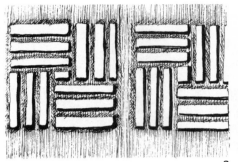

4

5

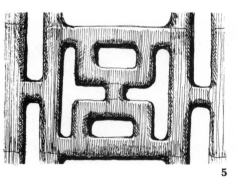

6

7

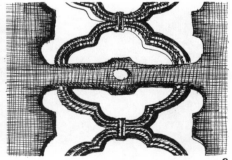

8

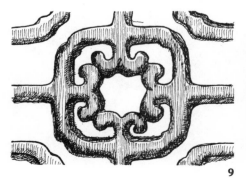

9

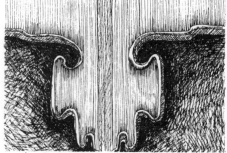

10

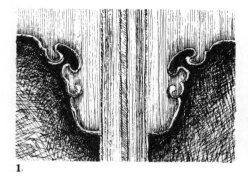

1.

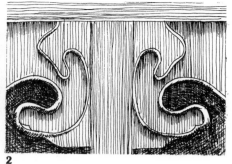

2

3

4

5

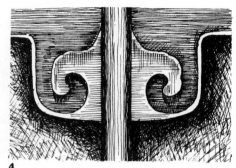

6

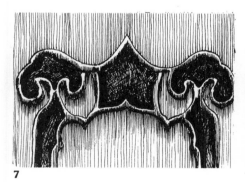

7

8

9

10

1. China—bench leg bracket; pierced and carved (seventeenth to eighteenth centuries).

2. China—skirt and leg bracket of a table (eighteenth century).

3. China—table motif; pierced and carved (eighteenth century).

4. China—bench leg bracket motif; built-up and relief-carved (eighteenth century).

5. China—side table stretcher; built-up and carved (eighteenth century).

6. China—heavy block foot of clothes stand; built-up and relief-carved (eighteenth century).

7. China—end of a side table; pierced and carved (eighteenth century).

8. China—characteristically Chinese design from toe-board or plinth for a wardrobe (eighteenth century).

9. China—wardrobe toe-board motif (eighteenth century).

10. China—motif from a chair splat; relief-carved (eighteenth century?).

1. China—Tibetan printing block; deep-cut knife and gouge work (nineteenth century).

2. Australia/Austral Islands—shield; chip-carved (eighteenth century).

1

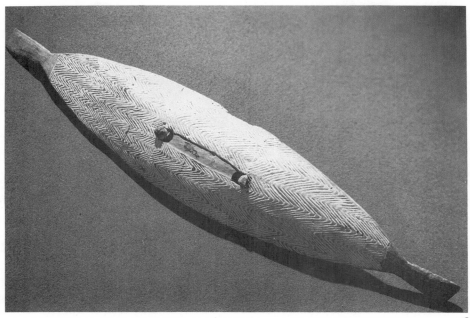

2

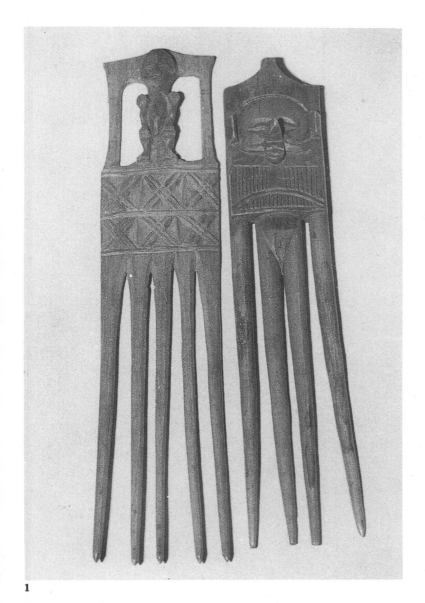

1

2

3

1. Africa—combs; chip-carved and pierced (twentieth century?).

2. Torres Strait—chip-carved, mastic-filled designs (eighteenth century).

3. Mexico—child's spinning top; knife-carved, stained, and incised pattern (nineteenth century).

Chapter 2

Circles

Oceanian Circles

1. New Guinea, Astrolabe Bay—shield motif; carved and painted (very early nineteenth century).

2. Trobriand Islands—canoe prow motif; carved in deep relief (nineteenth century).

3. New Guinea, Huon Gulf— knee-joint motif from a headrest carved in the form of a human figure; knife- and adze-carved (nineteenth century).

4. New Hebrides, Gaua—stylized "eye" motif from a fern tree figure; knife- and adze-carved (nineteenth century).

5. New Guinea, Lake Sentani—stylized "eye" motif taken from a figure on the carved ridge board of a house (nineteenth century).

6. New Guinea, Sepik District—"ear" detail from a ridge board figure; knife- and adze-carved (nineteenth century).

7. New Guinea, Lake Sentani—"ear" detail from a carved ridge board figure; knife- and adze-carved (nineteenth century).

8. New Guinea—carved decoration around the eyelet of a wooden fishing hook; knife- and adze-carved (nineteenth century).

9. New Hebrides—"eye" motif from a drum figure; knife- and adze-carved (nineteenth century).

10. Austral Islands, Raivavae—incised motif on the side of a domestic food bowl; early nineteenth century Oceanian carving was done with shell and stone tools since it was only in the late nineteenth century that iron tools were in general use (nineteenth century).

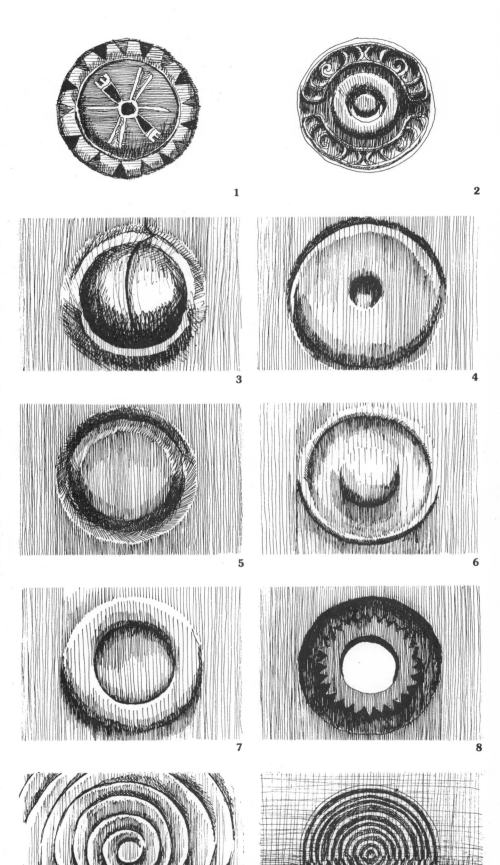

1

2

3

4

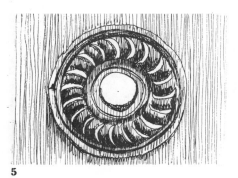

5

6

7

8

9

10

1. Oceania—decorative motif on a panel; knife-worked (nineteenth century?).

2. New Guinea—decorative motif on a domestic bowl; relief-carved (nineteenth century).

3. Solomon Islands—shield motif; carved and painted (nineteenth century).

4. Solomon Islands—dance shield motif; carved and painted, probably worked with stone adze and bone knife (nineteenth century).

5. Oceania—pierced motif from the handle of a lime spatula or pigment stick; knife-carved (nineteenth century?).

6. New Zealand (Maori)—"joint" motif from a large, carved door post figure; adze- and knife-carved (early nineteenth century).

7. New Caledonia—decorative motif from the head of a house post figure (nineteenth century).

8. New Guinea—"eye" motif from a carved and painted shield figure (nineteenth century).

9. Austral Islands—pattern detail from the rim of a carved food bowl; knife and gouge work (nineteenth century).

10. New Zealand (Maori)—knee joint motif from a relief-carved door lintel figure; probably carved with primitive stone and shell tools (eighteenth to nineteenth centuries).

59

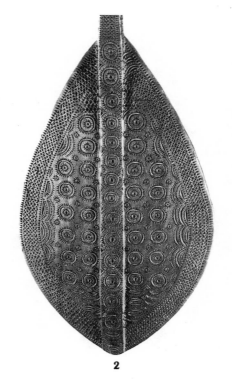

1. New Zealand (Maori)—part of a canoe prow; heavily carved and pierced, adze and knife work (eighteenth century).

2. Polynesia—paddle blade; shallow chip carving (eighteenth to nineteenth centuries).

3. Trobriand Islands—paddle blade patterned with incised line (eighteenth to nineteenth centuries).

4. Oceania—Fiji club; chip-carved (nineteenth century).

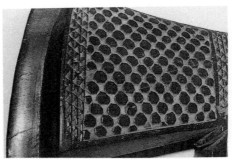

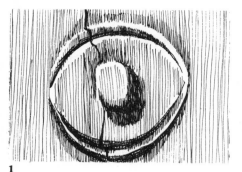

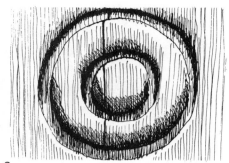

1

2

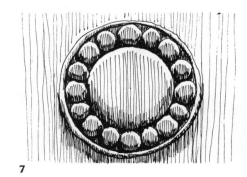

3

4

5

6

7

1. New Hebrides—"eye" motif from the underside of a domestic food dish; adze- and knife-carved (nineteenth century).

2. Trobriand Islands—lime spatula or pigment knife motif; knife-carved in shallow relief (nineteenth century).

3. New Guinea—death mask pendant; knife-carved and pierced (nineteenth century).

4. New Guinea—pendant from a myth figure; pierced, knife-carved, and painted (nineteenth century).

5. New Guinea—gable decoration; carved and painted (nineteenth century).

6. Solomon Islands, New Georgia—"ear ring" from a characteristic canoe prow figure; carved and shell-inlaid (nineteenth century).

7. New Guinea, Sepik District—ridge board motif; knife-carved (nineteenth century).

European Inlay and Marquetry

1. England—chair back motif; cut and inlaid with two woods (seventeenth century).

2. England—chair splat motif; cut and inlaid with two woods; the design shows an Oriental influence (seventeenth century).

3. Spain—inlaid cabinet motif; three woods are used (sixteenth century).

4. Netherlands—Dutch veneered bureau; very precise, highly polished work (eighteenth century).

5. England—"hare-wood" (dyed sycamore) commode motif; the design shows an Oriental influence (eighteenth century).

6. England—dressing table motif; cut and veneered (very early nineteenth century).

7. Spain—four wood inlaid motif from a Renaissance chest (sixteenth to seventeenth centuries).

8. England—Adam cabinet motif; very delicate, multicolored design (eighteenth century).

9. France—Louis XVI commode; four wood motif (eighteenth century).

10. England—motif from a mahogany hanging cabinet (early nineteenth century).

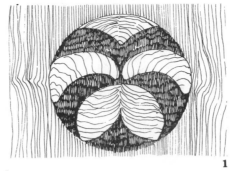

1

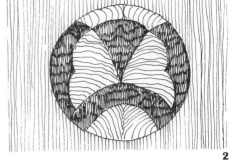

2

3

4

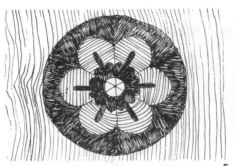

5

6

7

8

9

10

1. England—Chippendale bureau dressing table motif; pattern based on circular motifs (eighteenth century).

2. England—Adam sideboard motif (eighteenth century).

3. Italy—cassoni chest design; thick inlay (sixteenth century).

4. Netherlands—characteristic Dutch cabinet or cupboard motif (seventeenth century).

5. England—bookcase motif; thin, highly polished veneer (eighteenth century).

6. England—Hepplewhite motif, mahogany table (eighteenth century).

7. England—mahogany bureau dressing table; delicate, fine line, veneered motif (eighteenth century).

8. England—Pembroke table motif (eighteenth century).

9. Italy—cassoni chest motif; heavy inlay (sixteenth century).

10. Italy—motif inlaid with wood and shell (very early sixteenth century).

2

3

1

1. England—oak chest with characteristic chip-carved "rose" and twined circle designs; worked with gouge, chisel, and knife (sixteenth to seventeenth centuries).

2. England—butter markers; gouge work probably done by the village carver (nineteenth century).

3. Iceland—chip-carved bread stamp; compass-patterned motifs of this type are characteristic of eighteenth and nineteenth century north European carving (nineteenth century).

4. England, Leicestershire, Quenby Hall—chest motif; chip-carved "rose" and punched designs (early eighteenth century).

4

1

2

Chip Carving

1. Spain—Basque sideboard motif; shallow chip carving (eighteenth century).

2. Netherlands—Dutch spoon rack motif; simple but very organized chip-carved circle, with each depression achieved by making three chisel cuts (early nineteenth century).

3. Italy, Calabria—clothes beater motif; worked with knife, chisel, and gouge; although this motif looks complex, it can be broken down and achieved by a series of chip cuts (early eighteenth century).

4. Austria, Salzburg—mangle board motif; worked with chisel and knife; simple objects for use in the wash house and pantry were made by the village carpenter (eighteenth century).

5. Switzerland—clothes beater motif; the design is compass-based and chip-carved (eighteenth century).

3

4

5

Rose and Sun Circles

1. Norway—motif from the lid of a steamed and shaped pine box; knife-carved (eighteenth to nineteenth centuries).

2. Norway—butter mold motif; chip-carved circular design (nineteenth century).

3. Norway—six-part butter mold motif; chip-carved (nineteenth century).

4. Scandinavia—six-part chip-carved motif (eighteenth to nineteenth centuries).

5. Switzerland—hutch or chest motif; shallow chip-carved circle pattern on pine (thirteenth century).

1

2

3

4

5

1

2

3

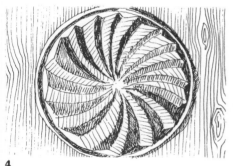

4

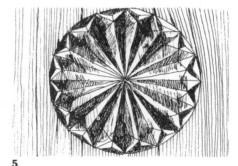

5

6

7

8

1. Albania—box lid; the box has been stained black and the motifs are based on chip-carved triangles (early nineteenth century).

2. England—chest motif (fourteenth century).

3. England—medieval pierced tracery motif from a livery cupboard; very crude chisel, gouge, and drill work (fifteenth century).

4. Norway—mangle board motif; these swirling, chip-carved circles are known as "roses" or "suns" (late eighteenth century).

5. Europe—carved "sun" motif; all the elements of the design are based on three cuts of the chisel (thirteenth century).

6. Spain—chest motif; deeply carved and undercut (fifteenth century).

7. Norway—fire screen chip-carved from a single slab of straight-grained pine; chisel, gouge, and knife work (seventeenth to eighteenth centuries).

8. England—oak chest motif; deeply cut and chip-carved with knife and chisel (thirteenth century).

Treen Carving

1. Germany—small table/stool motif; very shallow gouge carving (eighteenth century).

2. Norway—oak mangle motif; each element is achieved by three cuts of the chisel (nineteenth century).

3. Norway—oak mangle motif; shallow relief carving with knife and chisel (early nineteenth century).

4. England—traverse board; these peg boards, many of which were carved and decorated, were used to plot the course of a ship: the pegs were placed in the holes and were indications of compass bearings (eighteenth century).

5. Norway—oak mangle board motif; six-part design carved in shallow relief (seventeenth century).

6. Northern Europe—washing beater motif, "rose" or petal design; gouge- and knife-carved (eighteenth century).

7. Norway—pine mangle board design; heavy, rough, carved motif, not characteristic of other works of this period or area (nineteenth century).

8. Wales—loving spoon motif; pierced and carved in yew wood (eighteenth to nineteenth centuries).

9. Netherlands, Friesland—oak mangle board motif; six-part, carved, knife- and gouge-worked design (eighteenth century).

10. France—pierced boxwood comb, detail (sixteenth century).

1

2

3

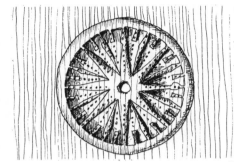

4

5

6

7

8

9

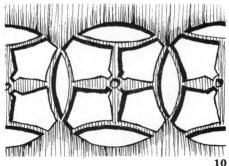

10

1

2

3

4

5

6

7

8

9

1. Scandinavia—oak ironing board motif; shallow chip carving with gouge and chisel (eighteenth century).

2. England—Tunbridgeware ruler motif; example of a curious inlay/veneer mosaic; three woods are used (eighteenth century).

3. Netherlands, Friesland—pine mangle board design; chip-carved with chisel and knife (eighteenth to nineteenth centuries).

4. England—Tunbridgeware measuring stick motif; four different-colored woods are used to make up this design (seventeenth to eighteenth centuries).

5. Scandinavia—tally board patterns; the triangles are characteristically chip-carved with three cuts of the chisel (eighteenth century).

6. England—Tunbridgeware mosaic circle motif; three different-colored woods are used to make up this design (eighteenth to nineteenth centuries).

7. England—Tunbridgeware games board motif; this mosaic design uses at least three different-colored woods (eighteenth to nineteenth centuries).

8. England—pine washboard motif; deeply chip-carved (nineteenth century).

9. England—Tunbridgeware games board motif; a good example of early work (eighteenth century).

European Folk Carving

1. England—ceiling boss (ornamental stud); deeply gouged and undercut; possibly carved as a "test" piece (fifteenth century).

2. England—chest motif; gouge-worked in shallow relief (sixteenth century).

3. Wales—pierced loving spoon motif based on radius arcs (nineteenth century).

4. England—carved printing block design (eighteenth century).

5. Germany—farmhouse wall panel, simple motif; gouge and chisel work; probably cut by the village carver (fifteenth century).

6. Switzerland—cup motif, a six-part design; worked in shallow relief (seventeenth century).

7. Sweden—corner cupboard motif; a six-part petal design (eighteenth to nineteenth centuries).

1

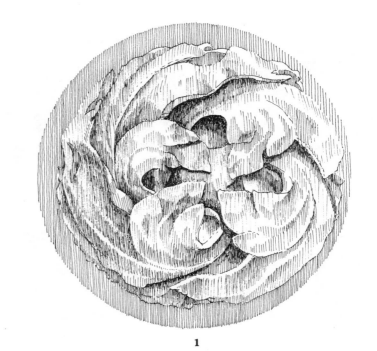

2

3

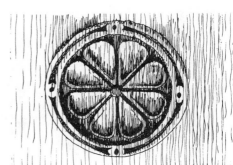

4

5

6

7

1

2

3

4

5

6

7

8

9

10

1. Switzerland—cupboard motif; chip-carved in pine wood (seventeenth century?).

2. Switzerland—cupboard motif; deeply chip-carved; the depressions are achieved by three cuts of the chisel (seventeenth century).

3. Switzerland—cupboard motif; carved with a fine gouge (seventeenth to eighteenth centuries).

4. Finland, East Bothnia—chest motif; shallow relief carving, worked with fine gouge on pine wood (nineteenth century).

5. Switzerland—cupboard motif; deep relief carving with chip carving at the circumference, worked in pine with chisel and gouge (nineteenth century).

6. Switzerland—furniture motif; deep undercut pattern; not characteristic of the work of this period or area (seventeenth to eighteenth centuries).

7. Switzerland—furniture motif; all of the elements of the carving are achieved by the use of three cuts of the chisel (eighteenth century).

8. Germany—farmhouse wall panel; worked with gouge and drill (fifteenth century).

9. Portugal—peasant-made ox yoke; this motif is shallowly chip-carved and brightly painted (nineteenth century).

10. Portugal—ox yoke motif; carved and painted (nineteenth century).

2

1

3

1. Italy—cittern (guitar) by Andra Taus, detail; pierced and carved with drill and gouge in a straight-grained, knot-free wood (seventeenth century).

2. Germany—detail of a cittern (guitar); pierced and gouged, worked with drill, gouge, and knife (seventeenth century).

3. Egypt, Cairo—pulpit; built-up, pierced, chip-carved, and painted (eighteenth century?).

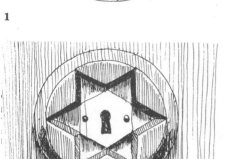

1

2

Middle Eastern Circles

1. Egypt—pierced and painted motif from a built-up and carved pulpit (eighteenth to nineteenth centuries).

2. Egypt—pulpit, detail; carved and painted (eighteenth to nineteenth centuries).

3. Spain—chest, detail; shallow relief, six-part star, with brass lock mount (late seventeenth century).

4. North Africa—pulpit/door, detail; carved, built-up, and painted (eighteenth century).

5. Persia—pierced motif from a ceremonial spoon; worked with gouge and drill (nineteenth century).

6. Turkey—Koran desk, detail; carved and inlaid (eighteenth century).

7. Egypt—Koran desk, detail; gouge-carved and inlaid (fourteenth century).

8. Persia—knife-carved ceremonial spoon, detail; chip-carved and incised (nineteenth century).

9. Spain—chest motif; chip-carved "rose" design; very characteristic of the period (seventeenth century).

10. Persia—pear wood spoon handle, very delicate, detailed design, detail; pierced and carved; the spoon was only used ceremonially (nineteenth century).

3

4

5

6

7

8

9

10

73

Folk and Treen Carving

1. Europe—oak chest, very basic depression and knob pattern, detail; gouge-carved (fifteenth century).

2. Norway—Romanesque chair motif; gouge- and knife-carved in pine (nineteenth century).

3. Germany—oak chest motif; shallow relief carving with adze and gouge (fifteenth century).

4. Northern Europe—oak washing bat or beater motif, characteristic "rose" design; worked with chisel and gouge (eighteenth century).

5. England—butter stamp motif; worked with knife and gouge in pine (eighteenth century).

6. England—butter stamp pattern; worked with knife and gouge in sycamore (eighteenth century).

7. England—busk or corset stiffener motif with a six-circle design; incised sycamore (eighteenth century).

8. Europe—Romanesque pine razor case motif; carved in shallow relief (nineteenth century).

9. England—wassail bowl motif; carved in sycamore and incised and stained (seventeenth century).

10. France—bread stamp; deeply embossed and carved (eighteenth century).

1

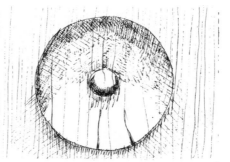

2

3

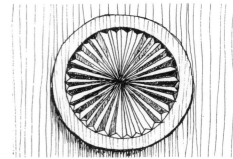

4

5

6

7

8

9

10

1. England—busk or corset stiffener motif; incised on sycamore (eighteenth century).

2. England—busk or corset stiffener motif; incised and chip-carved, worked with chisel and knife (seventeenth to eighteenth centuries).

3. England—butter stamp motif, unusual six-point star design; deeply chip-carved (eighteenth century).

4. Wales—busk love token design; incised and stained, worked with knife (eighteenth century).

5. Scandinavia—butter mold motif; worked with knife and gouge in sycamore (nineteenth century).

6. England—wassail bowl motif; worked on the lid with knife, gouge, and chisel (seventeenth century).

7. England—wassail bowl design; worked with knife and chisel on lignum vitae (seventeenth century).

8. England—wassail bowl motif; very delicate chisel and knife work (seventeenth century).

9. England—wassail bowl motif, extremely complex design; worked with chisel, gouge, and knife (seventeenth century).

10. England—wassail bowl motif, spiral design; worked in lignum vitae with knife and chisel (seventeenth century).

European Medieval

1. France—chest motif; relief-carved in oak, worked with gouge and adze (thirteenth century).

2. England—screen fragment, detail; deeply undercut, worked with gouge and adze (fourteenth century).

3. England—oak chest motif, characteristic six-point design; gouge and adze work (fourteenth century).

4. Germany—oak cupboard motif (fifteenth century).

5. France—chest motif; relief-carved, worked with gouge and adze (fifteenth century).

6. England, Norfolk, Thompson Church—pierced screen motif; drilled and gouge-worked in oak (fourteenth century).

7. France—chest motif; deeply relief-carved (thirteenth century).

8. England, Norfolk, Wilton Church—chest motif, six-part design; gouge-carved and undercut (fourteenth century).

9. England—church chest motif; worked in oak with gouge and adze (fourteenth century).

10. Germany—cup motif, a six-point design; worked with knife and fine gouge (fifteenth century).

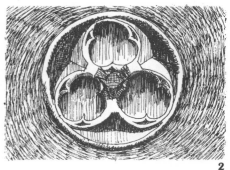

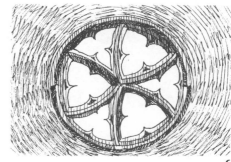

1

2

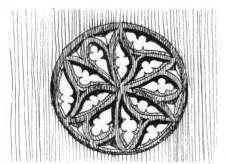

3

4

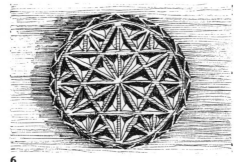

5

6

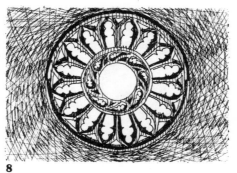

7

8

9

10

1. Germany—gable-roofed cupboard motif; deeply chip-carved in what looks like pine (fourteenth to fifteenth centuries).

2. Germany—tableware design; carved with knife and fine gouge (fifteenth century).

3. England, Norfolk—church screen, six-point design; pierced and gouge-worked in oak (fourteenth century).

4. Germany—drinking vessel motif; worked with knife and gouge (fifteenth century).

5. England, Norfolk—church screen; pierced and gouge-worked in oak (fourteenth century).

6. England—chip-carved chest, six-part circular design; each of the depressions is achieved by three cuts of the chisel (thirteenth century).

7. England—church screen; pierced and gouge-worked in oak (fourteenth century).

8. England, Norfolk—screen; pierced and gouge-worked (fourteenth century).

9. England—altar rail; pierced and gouge-worked (fourteenth century).

10. England—church screen motif; worked with drill, adze, and gouge (fourteenth century).

English Misericords

1. England, Wiltshire, Highworth Church—misericord supporter, detail; deeply carved and undercut, gouge and adze work (fifteenth century).

2. England, Kent, Herne Church—misericord supporter, detail; shallow relief-carved in oak (thirteenth to fourteenth centuries).

3. England, Cambridgeshire, Landbeach Church—foliated misericord, detail; gouge-carved in oak (thirteenth to fourteenth centuries).

4. England, Devonshire, Exeter Cathedral—misericord, detail, flower motif; carved in shallow relief (thirteenth to fourteenth centuries).

5. England, Norfolk, Great Doddington Church—misericord supporter, detail; gouge-carved and undercut in oak (fifteenth century).

6. England, Suffolk, Norton Church—misericord, detail, foliated design; gouge-carved in oak; not characteristic of other church carvings of this period (fourteenth century).

7. England, Cambridgeshire, Great Eversden Church—rose-shaped misericord supporter, detail; gouge-carved in oak (fifteenth century).

8. England, Northants, Holdenby Church—foliated misericord supporter, detail; not characteristic of other church carvings of this period; shallow gouge carving (fourteenth century).

9. England, Kent, Minister in Thanet—lion head misericord, detail; deeply gouge-carved and undercut (fifteenth century).

10. Scotland, Perth—misericord supporter, detail; chip-carved in oak (fourteenth to fifteenth centuries).

1

2

3

4

5

6

7

8

9

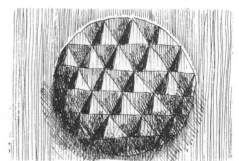

10

Spanish Furniture

1. Spain—chest motif; incised and chip-carved (thirteenth century).

2. Spain—chest motif, six-point design; carved in shallow relief (fifteenth century).

3. Spain—bench; pierced, drilled, and chip-carved (thirteenth to fourteenth centuries).

4. Spain—furniture pattern; carved in shallow relief, worked with gouge and chisel (fifteenth century).

5. Spain/England?—cupboard motif; carved in shallow relief (early sixteenth century).

6. Spain—chest pattern; worked in very shallow relief with adze and gouge (fifteenth century).

7. Spain—furniture design; gouge-worked in shallow relief (fifteenth century).

8. Spain—chest decoration; shallow relief and undercut (fifteenth century).

9. Spain—chest decoration, carved in shallow relief (fifteenth century).

10. Spain—chest decoration; gouge-carved in shallow relief (fifteenth century).

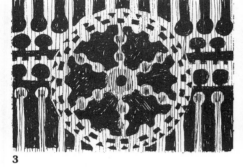

European Domestic Motifs

1. Sweden—washboard motif; shallow gouge cut, worked in a straight-grained pine (nineteenth century).

2. Netherlands—Dutch chest pattern; carved in shallow relief and undercut, worked with chisel and gouge (nineteenth century).

3. Finland—flax holder decoration; worked in shallow relief and pierced, knife work (nineteenth century).

4. Spain—chest motif; relief-worked and chip-carved, knife and gouge work (sixteenth to seventeenth centuries).

5. Norway—box decoration, incised six-point design; knife-worked in pine (eighteenth century).

6. Spain—cheese board decoration; chip-carved and incised, knife work (nineteenth century).

7. Netherlands—Dutch foot-warmer case decoration; delicately relief-carved and pierced (eighteenth century).

8. Spain—chest motif; characteristic peasant chip carving (seventeenth to eighteenth centuries).

9. Norway—wooden vessel motif; carved in shallow relief, knife worked (eighteenth century).

10. England—oak box motif; chip-carved, knife and chisel work (seventeenth to eighteenth centuries).

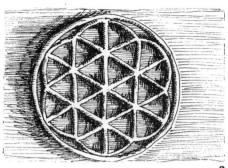

1

2

3

4

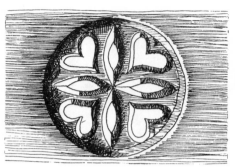

5

6

7

8

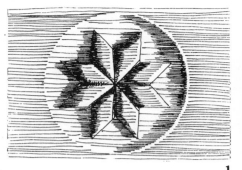

9

10

1. Belgium—furniture stand to be used in times of flood; slight relief work, pierced and chip-carved (eighteenth century).

2. England—oak casket motif; gouge-worked in shallow relief (fourteenth century).

3. Norway—bed end decoration; carved in low relief, worked with a knife (eighteenth century).

4. England—oak chest design; worked in shallow relief, undercut (fourteenth century).

5. Denmark—washboard decoration; chip-carved and incised, knife work (eighteenth century).

6. England—oak casket motif; low relief knife and gouge work (fourteenth century).

7. England—oak box motif; chip-carved and incised, knife and chisel work (seventeenth to eighteenth centuries).

8. England—box motif, six-point design; carved in shallow relief, worked with gouge (seventeenth to eighteenth centuries).

9. England—box motif; chip-carved and incised, worked with knife and chisel (eighteenth century).

10. England—casket design; delicately relief-carved and gouge-undercut (fourteenth century).

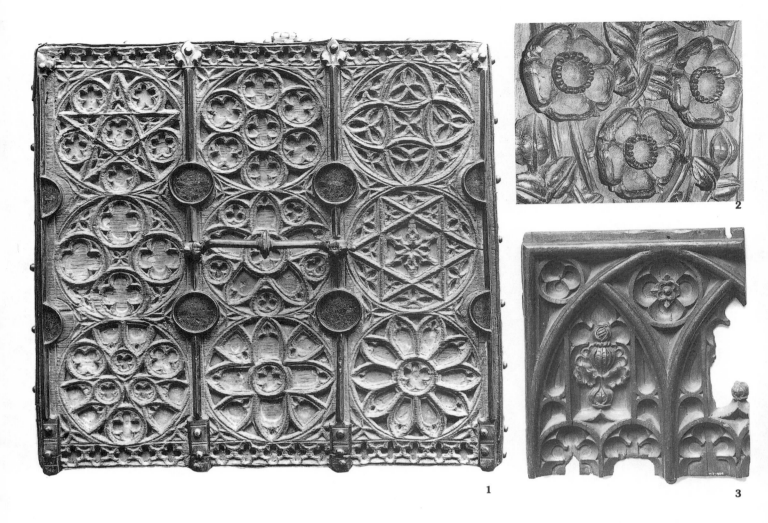

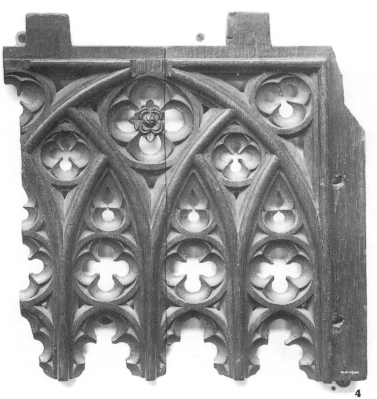

1. England—oak casket; delicate relief and deep gouge work (fourteenth century).

2. England—wall panel, detail; relief and gouge work (nineteenth to twentieth centuries).

3. England—Gothic oak tracery; relief and deep gouge work (fifteenth century).

4. England—oak tracery, probably part of a church screen; pierced and gouged (fifteenth century).

1

2

1. England, Salisbury—oak dole cupboard used to store provisions for the poor; pierced and gouge-worked (fifteenth century).

2. North Africa?—furniture detail; built-up, turned, and incised work (seventeenth to eighteenth centuries).

1. Persia—pearwood ceremonial spoons, pierced and chip-carved (nineteenth century).

2. South America, Brazil?—orlinda board; shallow gouge work and some slight relief carving (eighteenth to nineteenth centuries).

1

2

3

1. China—wood and lacquer dish, lotus flower design; in this particular instance the carved wood has been lacquer-coated and then incised (fourteenth century).

2. Japan—netsuke rat; three-dimensionally carved, probably with a knife (nineteenth century).

3. China—wood and lacquer box; gouge work; in this particular instance it is only the lacquer layers that are carved (fourteenth century).

Chapter 3

Twined Forms

Scrolls

1. England—cabinet, detail; relief-carved, gilded surface (mid-eighteenth century).

2. England—side table, detail; chisel and gouge work, gilded surface (eighteenth century).

3. England—table, detail; chisel and gouge work, gilded surface (eighteenth century).

4. England—cabinet, detail; chisel-worked and gilded (eighteenth century).

5. England—table, detail; chisel-carved and surface-gilded (eighteenth century).

6. England—table, detail; chisel-worked and gilded (mid-eighteenth century).

7. Italy—cassoni chest, detail; chisel-worked, the surface gilded (sixteenth century).

8. England—table, detail; chisel-carved and gilded, cut-away surface painted black (eighteenth century).

9. China—bed balustrade, swastika pattern, detail; pierced and deeply gouged (sixteenth century).

10. Spain—chair, detail; chisel-carved and gilded (eighteenth century).

1. England—library table, detail; relief-carved, gouge and chisel work (eighteenth century).

2. England—console table, detail; delicately carved and gilded, gouge and chisel work (eighteenth century).

3. England—library table, detail; gouge-carved and slightly undercut (eighteenth century).

4. England—chair, detail; carved in shallow relief and gilded (eighteenth century).

5. England—court cupboard, detail; stained and gilded (seventeenth century).

6. Germany—cupboard, detail; carved in low relief, chisel and gouge work (sixteenth century).

7. England—mirror, detail, ball and tongue pattern; gouge- and chisel-worked (eighteenth century).

8. Italy—cassoni chest, detail; deep chisel and gouge work (sixteenth century).

9. England—mirror frame, detail; traditional ball and tongue design; chisel and gouge work (eighteenth century).

10. France—commode, detail; worked with a gouge, with the cut-away surface stained black and the raised surface gilded (eighteenth century).

Plait and Twist

1. New Guinea, Sepik District—drum pattern; knife- and adze-carved, background lime-painted white (nineteenth century).

2. New Guinea, Sepik District—roof support of cult house, detail; worked with bone knives and shell adzes, then painted (nineteenth century).

3. Africa, Congo River Area—goblet handle, detail; knife-carved and then painted (nineteenth century).

4. Africa, Congo River Area (Bakuba)—pattern from the body area of a royal statue, detail; carved and painted, knife and adze work (nineteenth century).

5. Germany—Alpine chest decoration; carved in shallow relief (sixteenth century).

6. France—chest pattern; very shallow relief carving, worked with knife and gouge (fifteenth century).

1. Africa, Congo River Area (Bakuba)—royal statue pattern, base decoration; knife- and adze-carved (nineteenth century).

2. Cameroons—knife handle, detail; shallow knife-carved pattern (nineteenth century).

3. Italy—chair back, detail; pierced, knife and gouge work (sixteenth century).

4. Africa, Congo River Area—relief pattern from a small box; knife-worked (eighteenth to nineteenth centuries).

5. Mexico (Aztec)—relief-carved motif from a ceremonial drum; knife- and adze-carved (fifteenth century?).

Twined Chair Motifs

1. England—chair leg decoration; carved, fretted, and backed; worked with fine saws and needle files (eighteenth century).

2. England—chair stretcher design; pierced, fretted, and carved, worked with saws and chisels (eighteenth century).

3. England—chair design; pierced and fretted; this pattern is very characteristic of English furniture of the period (eighteenth century).

4. England—chair stretcher design; pierced, fretted, and backed (eighteenth century).

5. England—chair back motif; pierced and gouge-carved (seventeenth century).

6. England—chair stretcher motif; shallow, flat, carved work (mid-eighteenth century).

7. England—chair back, detail; built-up, pierced, and carved (eighteenth century).

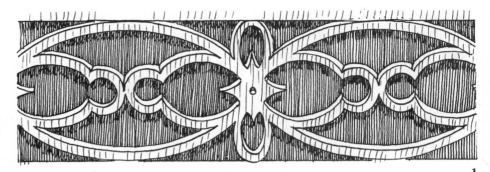

1

2

3

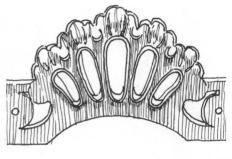

4

5

6

7

1

2

3

4

1. England, Leicestershire, Quenby Hall—Jacobean flat-carved wall panel; worked with chisel, gouge, and punch (early seventeenth century).

2. England—Jacobean pulpit, detail; flat strap work, gouged and punched (seventeenth century).

3. France—pearwood mandora (mandolin), detail; pierced, chiselled, and knife-worked (seventeenth century).

4. England, Leicestershire, Quenby Hall—Jacobean four-poster bed molding; worked with planes and gouges (early seventeenth century).

1. New Zealand (Maori)—feather box; adze-worked and chip-carved (nineteenth century?).

2. New Zealand—ceremonial spears; adze-worked and chip-carved (eighteenth to nineteenth centuries).

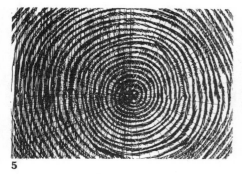

Spiral and Coil

1. New Hebrides—drum, detail; adze- and knife-worked, incised and chip-carved (nineteenth century).

2. New Zealand (Maori)—door post, detail; knife- and adze-worked (nineteenth century).

3. New Zealand (Maori)—prow of a war canoe, detail; pierced and deeply carved, worked with adze, drill, and knife (nineteenth century).

4. New Zealand (Maori)—manaia house frieze, detail; deeply adze- and knife-carved (eighteenth to nineteenth centuries).

5. New Zealand (Maori)—door post fragment, detail; knife-carved knee joint motif from a manaia figure (eighteenth to nineteenth centuries).

6. New Zealand, (Maori)—feather box decoration; adze and knife work (nineteenth century).

7. New Zealand (Maori)—characteristic Maori carving from the early period; worked with adze and knife (eighteenth to nineteenth centuries).

8. New Zealand (Maori)—manaia frieze, detail; adze- and knife-worked (nineteenth century).

9. New Guinea—canoe prow fragment; adze, drill, and knife work (nineteenth century).

10. Chile, Hermite Island—handle of a wooden cooking skewer, detail; pierced and carved (nineteenth century).

New Guinea
Twined

1. New Guinea—characteristic weapon motif; adze-carved and then painted (nineteenth century).

2. New Guinea—shield decoration; carved in shallow relief with adze and knife and painted with lime (nineteenth century).

3. New Guinea—motif from spear handle; human-form figures are knife-carved and then polished (nineteenth century).

4. New Guinea—motif from dance pole handle; shallow-carved and painted (nineteenth century).

5. New Guinea—weapon decoration, "insect"-type pattern; adze- and knife-worked and then painted (nineteenth century).

6. New Guinea—shield border pattern, knife-worked (nineteenth century).

7. New Guinea—crude weapon decoration; adze- and knife-worked and lime-painted (nineteenth century).

8. New Guinea—weapon design; knife-worked (nineteenth century).

9. New Guinea—shield border design; carved in shallow relief and painted (nineteenth century).

10. New Guinea—motif from fine, complex, knife-carved weapon (nineteenth century).

1

2

3

4

5

6

7

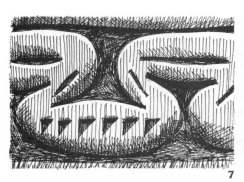

8

9

10

1

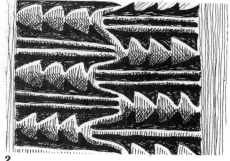

2

3

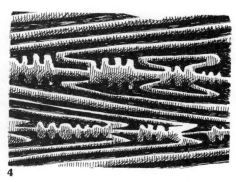

4

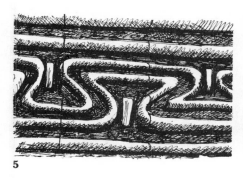

5

6

7

8

9

10

1. New Guinea—typical border frieze pattern for weapon; carved and sometimes painted (nineteenth century).

2. New Guinea—human-form pattern around the handle of a dance pole; very fine knife-carved work (nineteenth century).

3. New Guinea—pattern used on weapons and domestic items; shallow adze and knife carving (nineteenth century).

4. New Guinea—human-form design on the shaft of a spear; knife-carved and polished (nineteenth century).

5. New Guinea—border pattern from a shield; knife-carved and painted (nineteenth century).

6. New Guinea—weapon design; shallowly knife-carved, rounded, and painted (nineteenth century).

7. New Guinea—characteristic motif used on all manner of weapons and domestic items; knife-carved and sometimes painted (nineteenth century).

8. New Guinea—shield border decoration; adze- and knife-worked, sometimes painted (nineteenth century).

9. New Guinea—weapon decoration; adze- and knife-worked (nineteenth century).

10. New Guinea—weapon decoration; adze- and knife-worked (nineteenth century).

New Guinea Convoluted

1. New Guinea—drum motif; knife-carved and painted with white lime (nineteenth century).

2. New Guinea (Asmat)—shield decoration; deeply carved and painted, worked with adze and knife; early nineteenth century carving was achieved with stone and bone tools (nineteenth century).

3 and **4.** New Guinea—lime spatula or paint stick decoration; knife-carved (nineteenth century).

5. New Guinea (Asmat)—shield decoration; relief-carved and painted (nineteenth century).

6. New Guinea (Korwar)—shield motif; relief-carved and painted (nineteenth century).

7. New Guinea (Asmat)—shield decoration; carved and painted (nineteenth century).

8. New Guinea—weapon motif; adze- and knife-carved (nineteenth century).

9. New Guinea—shield border pattern, knife-carved (nineteenth century).

1

2

3

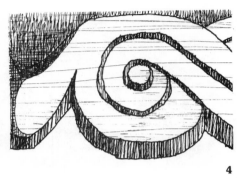
4

5

6

7

8

9

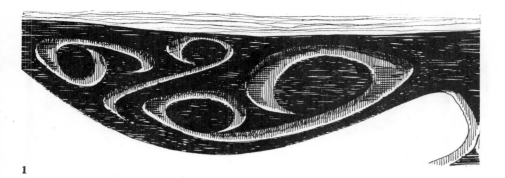

1

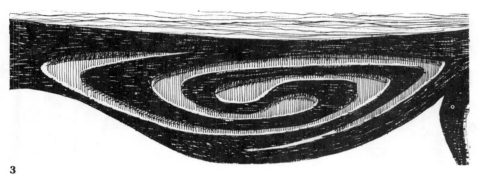

2

3

4

5

1. New Guinea, Lake Sentani—house roof apex or ridge board, detail; deep adze and knife work, sometimes painted (nineteenth century).

2. New Guinea, Lake Sentani—base of a domestic dish, detail; flat knife work (nineteenth century).

3. New Guinea, Lake Sentani—house roof apex or ridge board; deeply adze- and knife-carved (nineteenth century).

4. New Guinea, Lake Sentani—central house post design, detail; very complex, characteristic adze, knife, and bone gouge work, sometimes painted (nineteenth century).

5. New Guinea, Lake Sentani—drum pattern; carved in shallow relief and painted, worked with knife (nineteenth century).

Oceanian Convoluted

1. New Guinea—pattern from the shaft of a mortar or betel pounder; carved in shallow relief and polished, worked with adze and knife (nineteenth century).

2. New Guinea, Geelvink Bay—canoe prow, pierced and carved, heavy adze and knife work (nineteenth century).

3. Trobriand Islands—lime spatula handle; relief-carved and painted, fine knife work (nineteenth century).

4. Trobriand Islands—handle of a lime spatula, detail; knife-carved and painted (nineteenth century).

5. New Guinea, Sepik District—motif from a carved and painted shield; worked with adze and knife (nineteenth century).

6. New Guinea, Sepik District—shield motif; carved and painted (nineteenth century).

7. New Guinea—pattern from a wooden fishing hook, detail (nineteenth century).

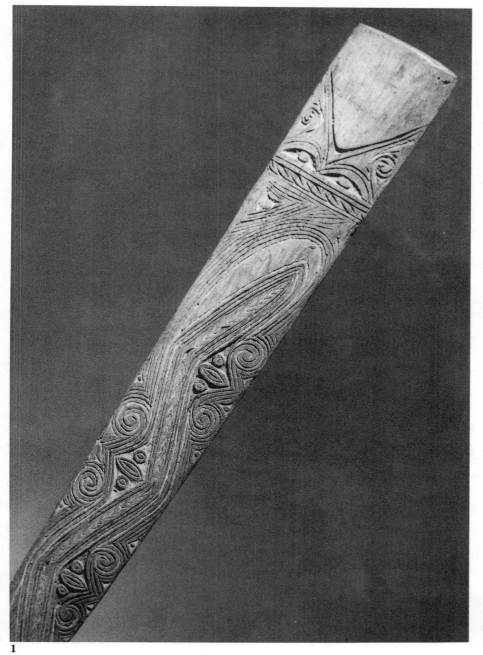

1. New Ireland—paddle blade; chip-carved, adze-worked, and knife-carved (nineteenth century).

2. New Guinea—war club; adze- and knife-worked, incised, patterned, and mastic-filled design (nineteenth century?).

Repeat Twined

1. England—box settle (high-backed bench seat); incised and shallow-carved decoration, worked with gouge and chisel (seventeenth century).

2. Netherlands—Dutch cupboard decoration; relief-carved, gouge and chisel work (seventeenth century).

3. England—snuff rasp (used in grinding snuff), detail; fine knife and gouge work (eighteenth century).

4. Netherlands—Dutch cupboard motif; gouge and chisel work (seventeenth century).

5. France—high-backed seat, detail; flat-carved, worked with gouge and chisel (sixteenth century).

6. England—snuff rasp decoration; knife-incised (eighteenth century).

7. England—incised pattern on a chalice; knife-worked (seventeenth century).

8. England—snuff box pattern; incised and knife-worked (eighteenth century).

9. England—chalice decoration; incised knife work (seventeenth century).

10. England—wooden tableware decoration; scratched or incised work (seventeenth century).

1

2

3

4

5

6

7

8

9

10

1

3

2

4

5

6

7

1. Indonesia, Tanimbar District—decoration from the head area of a sculpture; deep relief gouge work (eighteenth to nineteenth centuries).

2. Europe—box; carved in shallow relief, worked with knife, chisel, and gouge (thirteenth century).

3. France—church bench decoration; pierced and gouge-worked (fourteenth century).

4. Europe—box; shallow gouge work (thirteenth century).

5. Europe—box chest; shallow gouge and chisel work (thirteenth century).

6. England—chest; flat-carved, worked with chisel and gouge (seventeenth century).

7. England—chest; chip-carved and worked in shallow relief with knife and gouge (fifteenth century).

1. India, Madras, Kerala Border—teak lattice window of interlaced cobras; pierced, gouged, and chip-carved (seventeenth century).

2. Burma—monastery gates made from heavy teak slabs; deep relief gouge, chisel, knife, and drill work (sixteenth to seventeenth centuries).

3. India, Madras, Kerala Border—teak gable end; built-up and gouge-worked (sixteenth century).

4. India—door pillar capital; adze, knife, and gouge work (seventeenth century).

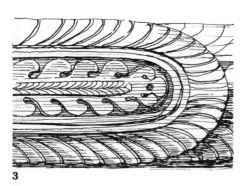

1

2

Foliated Twined

1. Burma—gate decoration; gouge, chisel, drill, and knife work (seventeenth century).

2. India—motif taken from roof gable, detail; worked with gouge, chisel, and knife (sixteenth century).

3. Burma—gate motif; chisel and gouge work (seventeenth century).

4. Burma—teak monastery doors, detail; knife and gouge work, deeply undercut (seventeenth century).

5. India, Jaipur—door post; deep gouge work (seventeenth to eighteenth centuries).

6. India, Jaipur—door pillar; deep chisel and gouge work (seventeenth to eighteenth centuries).

7. Portugal—box chest; flat-carved, worked with gouge (eighteenth century).

8. Italy, Sardinia—chest, detail; shallow gouge carving (seventeenth century).

9. Portugal—chest, detail; carved in shallow relief and chip-worked with knife and gouge (seventeenth century).

10. Italy—chair, detail; gouge-worked and slightly undercarved (sixteenth century).

3

4

5

6

7

8

9

10

European Twined

1. Germany—cupboard decoration; flat-carved in low relief, gouge- and chisel-carved (fifteenth century).

2. Switzerland—bed; flat-carved in low relief, gouged and chisel-carved (sixteenth century).

3. Germany—box settle; flat-carved in low relief (fifteenth century).

4. Germany—Alpine cupboard, detail; chisel- and gouge-worked (sixteenth century).

5. Germany—cupboard; gouge- and chisel-worked in soft pine (early sixteenth century).

1

2

3

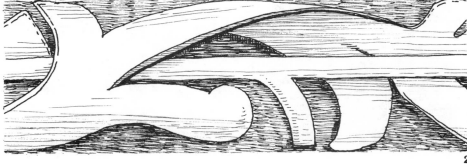

4

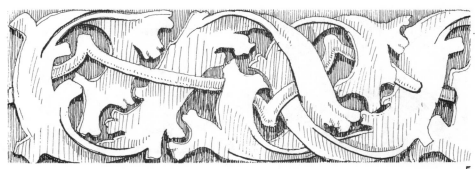

5

1. Switzerland—bed decoration; gouge-worked and background-punched (sixteenth century).

2. Switzerland—bed, detail; gouge and chisel work (sixteenth century).

3. Switzerland—bed, detail; chisel- and gouge-worked in pine (sixteenth century).

4. Germany—chest, detail; flat-carved in low relief with chisel and gouge (fifteenth century).

Twined Chair Motifs

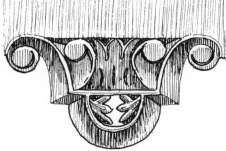

1. England—chair stretcher; carved and pierced (seventeenth century).

2. England—chair back, detail; pierced and gouge-worked (seventeenth century).

3. England—chair back, detail; gouge-carved and incised (late seventeenth century).

4. England—chair back, detail; built-up, pierced, and gouge-carved (seventeenth century).

5. England—chair back, detail; pierced, gouge-carved, and turned (late seventeenth century).

6. England—chair back, detail; relief-carved, worked with gouge and chisel (late seventeenth century).

7. England—top of chair back, detail; carved in low relief, worked with gouge and chisel (seventeenth century).

8. England—chair back; built-up, carved, worked with gouge and chisel, turned work added (seventeenth century).

9. Spain—chair stretcher, detail; deeply gouge-carved and pierced (early eighteenth century).

10. Spain—chair seat, detail; gouge-worked (eighteenth century).

1

2

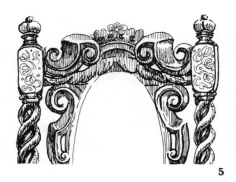

3

4

5

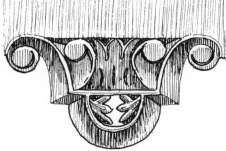

6

7

8

9

10

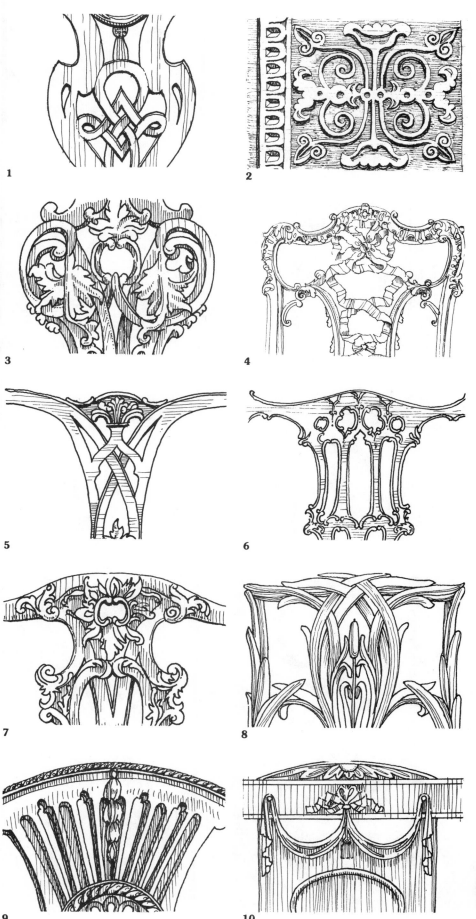

1. England—chair back; pierced, fretted, and gouge-carved (eighteenth century).

2. England—chair back decoration; flat relief-carved, chip-carved, and punch-textured (seventeenth century).

3. England—chair back; pierced, fretted, and gouge-carved (seventeenth century).

4. England—chair back, ribbon motif; built-up, fretted, worked with saw, gouge, and drill (mid-eighteenth century).

5. England—chair back; pierced and flat-carved, fretted and gouged (mid-eighteenth century).

6. England—chair back, detail; built-up, pierced, and gouge-carved (eighteenth century).

7. England—chair back; built-up, glued, fretted, and gouge-carved (mid-eighteenth century).

8. England—chair back, detail; gouge- and chisel-carved (eighteenth century).

9. England—chair back; built-up and gouge-carved, worked with saws, drills, and gouges (eighteenth century).

10. England—chair back (eighteenth century).

Western Twined, Flat-Carved, and Inlaid

1. Europe—door panel; flat-carved, cut-away ground, chisel and gouge work (sixteenth century).

2. United States—Colonial(?) cupboard motif; flat-carved, cut-away ground, chisel and gouge work (seventeenth century).

3. England—bed decoration, detail; carved in flat relief, shallow gouge work (seventeenth century).

4. United States—Colonial cupboard motifs; flat-carved, cut-away ground, chisel and gouge work (seventeenth century).

5. France—cupboard panel, detail, strap motif; cut-away ground, worked with gouge and chisel (seventeenth century).

1. England—inlay panel using two different types of wood (sixteenth century).

2. Portugal—panel; ebony and ivory inlay, pinned and glued (early seventeenth century).

3. England—cuboard inlay panel; cut and worked with two types of wood (sixteenth century).

4. Switzerland—chest inlay, detail; marquetry using two wood types (seventeenth century).

5. Czechoslovakia, Bohemia—cupboard, detail; thick marquetry using two wood types (seventeenth century).

Scandinavian Convoluted

1. Norway—large wooden bowl, rim detail; knife-worked (eighteenth century).

2. Norway—Romanesque plaited motif from a cupboard door; knife and adze work (thirteenth century).

3. Norway—house door post; deep gouge and knife work (fourteenth century).

4. Norway—box/chest, detail; flat-carved with chisel and gouge, worked in a smooth-grained, knot-free pine (eighteenth century).

5. Northern Europe(?)—box decoration; rough adze and knife work (thirteenth century).

6. Iceland—cupboard, detail; relief-carved motif, adze and knife work (fourteenth century?)

7. Iceland—chair back motif; gouge and knife work, relief-carved (fifteenth century).

1. Norway—box chest, detail; flat relief-carved and chip-carved (seventeenth century).

2. Norway—door post pattern; flat-carved (eighteenth century).

3. Iceland—chest motif; flat-carved and incised with adze, gouge, and knife work (fourteenth century?).

4. Norway—large wool chest, detail; carved in shallow relief and chip-carved; characteristic of Norwegian peasant carving (fourteenth to fifteenth centuries).

5. Norway—door post, detail; flat relief work and chip carving (fourteenth century).

6. Norway, Urnes, Stave Church—wall panel; relief-carved and slight undercut work with adze, gouge, and knife (pre-eleventh century?).

113

Viking

1. Norway, Setesdal, Hylestad Church—Sigurdr kills the dragon Fafnir; flat relief, adze and gouge work (twelfth century).

2. Norway, Setesdal, Hylestad Church—carving that illustrates the tale of Sigurdr and the dragon, detail; adze and gouge work (twelfth century).

3. Norway, Urnes—gable detail from the Urnes stave or plank-built church; adze and gouge work, relief work, slightly undercut (pre-eleventh century).

1

2

3

1

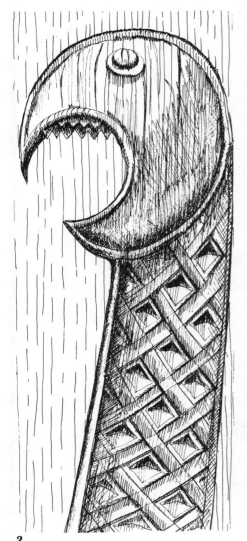

2

3

1. Norway—Viking ship's figurehead; three-dimensionally worked with adze and gouge, some chip-carved decoration (ninth to tenth centuries).

2. Norway—pre-Viking ship's figurehead; three-dimensionally adze- and gouge-carved and deeply chip-carved.

3. Norway, Osberg Ship Mound—Viking ship's figurehead, detail; adze and gouge relief-carved (ninth century).

Viking Animalistic Twined

1. Norway, Setesdal, Hylestad Church—story of Sigurdr and the dragon carved in wood; in this detail Sigurdr is roasting the dragon's heart; adze- and gouge-worked (twelfth century).

2. Norway, Urnes, Stave Church—in this detail Yggdrasill is being gnawed by the hart, Eicbyrmr; deeply rounded relief carving, adze and gouge work (pre-eleventh century).

3. Norway, Osberg Ship Mound—ship's figure-head; three-dimensionally adze- and gouge-carved (ninth century).

4. Norway—medieval wool box/chest, detail; carved in flat relief and decorated with chip carving.

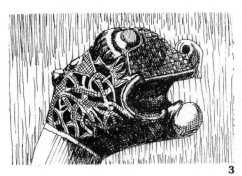

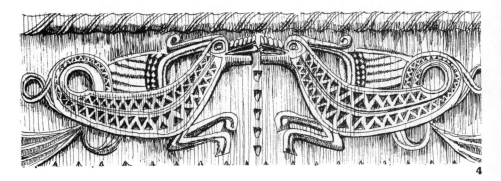

116

1. Norway—tankard; cooper-built, strapped, and relief-carved, shallow gouge work (eighteenth century).

2. Germany—tankard; deep gouge, naturalistic carving and brass stud work (seventeenth century).

3. Switzerland—cupboard, detail; flat-carved, worked with gouge and knife (sixteenth century).

4. Iceland—panel; flat relief gouge work (early nineteenth century).

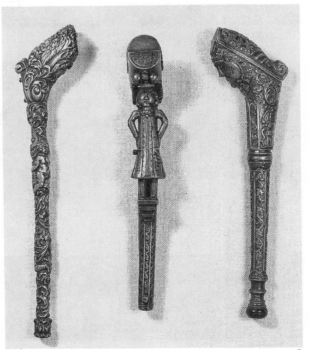

1. England—oak panel; deep gouge work (sixteenth century).

2. England—violin/viola with the Royal coat of arms; built-up and gouge-carved (seventeenth century).

3. Netherlands—Dutch pipe cases; naturalistic gouge work (seventeenth century).

1

2

3

1. Italy—closet or small room, panelled in white and gilded; gouge-carved panels (eighteenth century).

2. England—art nouveau panel; deeply relief-carved and undercut, worked with gouge and chisel (late nineteenth century).

3. France—walnut art nouveau armchair carved by Louis Marjdrelle; built-up and gouge-carved, highly polished finish (twentieth century).

Chapter 4

Plant Forms

Fleur-de-Lys and Related Forms

1. France—chest motif; flat-carved with cutaway ground, worked with gouge and chisel (thirteenth century).

2. Germany—chest motif; carved in very flat relief (sixteenth century).

3. Germany—cupboard top, detail; pierced and fretted, some gouge work (fifteenth century).

4. England—cupboard, detail; inlay/marquetry using two wood types (sixteenth century).

5. Italy—chest motif; relief-carved, gouge and knife work (fifteenth century).

6. Portugal—cabinet, detail; inlay worked in ebony, oak, and ivory (seventeenth century).

7. Italy—bench seat motif; carved in shallow relief, chisel and gouge work (sixteenth century).

8. Germany—table decoration, detail; worked in low relief (eighteenth century).

9. England—cupboard, detail; carved in deep relief and undercut, gouge and chisel work (sixteenth century).

10. Spain—heavy relief-carved motif; worked with adze and gouge (sixteenth century).

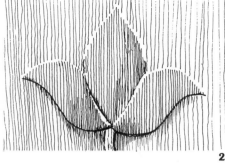

1

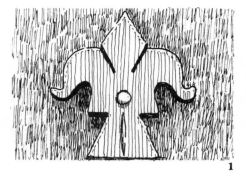

2

3

4

5

6

7

8

9

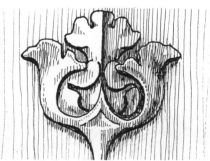

10

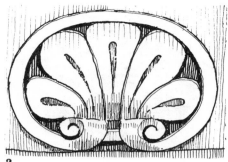

1

2

Honeysuckle and Shell

1. Spain—cabinet, detail; worked in high relief (seventeenth century).

2. Italy, Rome—cassoni chest, detail; worked with gouge and knife (mid-sixteenth century).

3. France—cupboard, detail; gouge-carved (sixteenth century).

4. France—cupboard, detail; gouge-worked and undercut (sixteenth century).

5. Italy—wooden column motif; adze-worked and ground cut away (twelfth century).

6. Italy—church choir stalls, detail; built-up, gouge-worked, and undercut (sixteenth century).

7. England—Adam style chair back, detail; pierced and fretted (eighteenth century).

8. Germany—design from the back of a carpenter's long plane; gouge-carved in flat relief (early nineteenth century).

9. England—Chippendale desk motif; worked in marquetry using two types of wood (eighteenth century).

10. Germany—carpenter's plane motif; shallow gouge-carving (early nineteenth century).

3

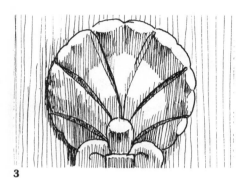

4

5

6

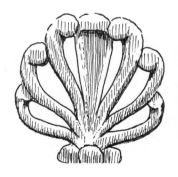

7

8

9

10

Foliated Scroll

1. United States—motif from a slipper chair; three-dimensionally gouge-carved (mid-nineteenth century).

2. France, Alsace—butter stamp; chip-carved, worked with a knife (nineteenth century).

3. France—armchair, detail; three-dimensionally worked with saw and gouge (sixteenth century).

4. Italy, Calabria—clothes beater decoration; chip-carved, worked with gouge and knife (eighteenth century).

5. France—commode, detail; built-up and gouge-carved (eighteenth century).

6. Burma—motif from a temple gate; adze- and knife-carved (sixteenth to seventeenth centuries).

7. England—wall lantern bracket; three-dimensionally carved, gilded (eighteenth century).

8. Spain—flax swingle or holder; thin flat wood, pierced, fretted, and chip-carved (nineteenth century).

9. France—writing table; three-dimensionally gouge-carved and then pinned and glued onto the table (mid-eighteenth century).

10. Persia—ceremonial spoon, detail; pierced and fretted (nineteenth century).

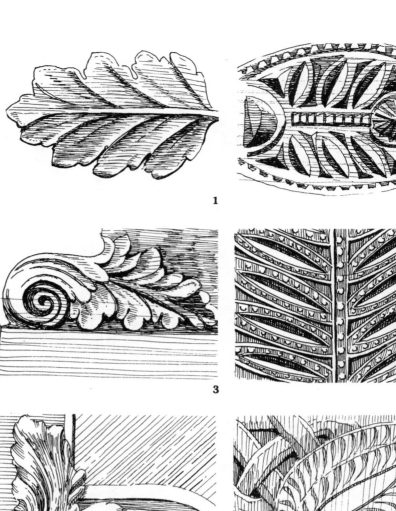

1

2

3

4

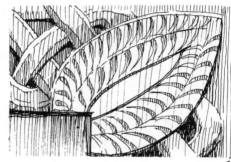

5

6

7

8

9

10

1

2

3

4

5

6

7

8

9

10

1. England—high-backed chair, detail of the cut-away ground-pattern; worked with gouge and chisel (seventeenth century).

2. Italy, Venice—chest motif; carved in deep relief and gilded, worked with gouge and chisel (sixteenth century).

3. Iceland—cupboard door, detail, traditional design; carved in flat relief, gilded cut-away ground (seventeenth century).

4. England, Leicestershire, Quenby Hall—Jacobean wall panel, detail, low relief-carved "strapwork" motif; worked with gouge and chisel (seventeenth century).

5. England—court cupboard, detail; carved in shallow relief, worked with gouge and chisel (seventeenth century).

6. England—chair back decoration; shallow flat-relief work with gouge and chisel (sixteenth century).

7. India, Madras—gable, detail; deep gouge carving, slightly undercut, worked with adze and knife (sixteenth century).

8. England—bench/table pattern, detail; flat-carved and incised (seventeenth century).

9. England—chair back; pierced and gouge-carved (seventeenth century).

10. England—chair border decoration; gouge-carved and incised (sixteenth century).

Curled Leaf

1. Switzerland—pine cupboard; carved in low relief with cut-away ground, chisel- and gouge-worked (sixteenth century).

2. Mexico (Spanish)—set of domestic measures; carved in low relief and incised, knife work (eighteenth century).

3. England—oak cupboard panel; undercut almost three-dimensionally, worked with shaped gouges (sixteenth century).

4. England—furniture panel, wild rose leaf motif; gouge- and chisel-worked (nineteenth century).

5. England—Jacobean four-poster bed decoration; carved in low relief and incised (seventeenth century).

6. England—Grinling Gibbons mirror frame; built-up, gouge-carved, and glued (seventeenth century).

7. England—Elizabethan(?) furniture panel, nut motif; relief-carved with chisel and knife (sixteenth century).

8. France—screen by Emile Galle; built-up, pierced, and carved (late nineteenth century).

9. Mexico (Spanish)—domestic bowl motif; carved in low relief and incised, gouge and knife work (eighteenth century).

10. France(?)—throne chair, detail; built-up, carved, painted, and gilded (nineteenth century).

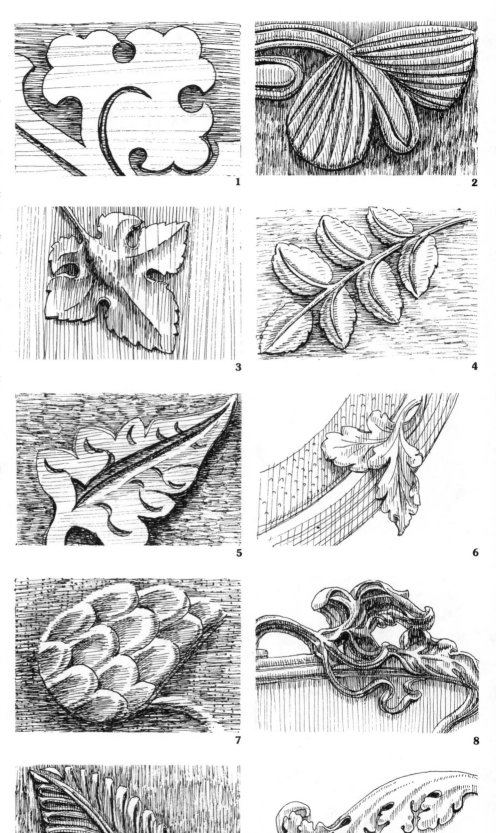

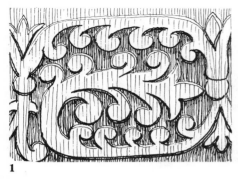

1

2

3

4

5

6

7

8

9

10

1. Norway—tankard pattern; flat knife carving (eighteenth century).

2. Italy—wooden column decoration; simple adze and gouge work (twelfth century).

3. Italy, Salerno—column capital decoration; adze and gouge work (twelfth century).

4. England—Jacobean pulpit decoration; flat strap-work, the ground cut away (seventeenth century).

5. Mexico (Spanish)—domestic bowl pattern; low relief knife-work (eighteenth century).

6. France—throne chair; built-up, carved, painted, and gilded (nineteenth century?).

7. Netherlands—Dutch pipe case decoration; acanthus leaf motif; knife-carved (seventeenth century).

8. England—bookcase, detail; three-dimensionally carved, glued, worked with knife and gouge (nineteenth century).

9. England—musical instrument, detail; carved in deep relief and undercut (seventeenth century).

10. England—mahogany chest, detail; built-up, pierced, and gouge-carved (eighteenth century).

European Pierced and Relif

1. Norway—spoon handle, detail; pierced and knife-worked (nineteenth century).

2. Norway—tankard handle; built-up, pierced, and knife-carved (nineteenth century).

3. Norway—ironing board pattern; gouged and knife-worked (eighteenth century).

4. Norway—tankard handle; built-up, pierced, and carved, worked with knife (nineteenth century).

5. Norway—travel trunk, detail; deep relief carving, slightly undercut, worked with knife and gouge (eighteenth century).

6. Norway—Rococo cupboard motif; worked in deep relief and pierced (eighteenth century).

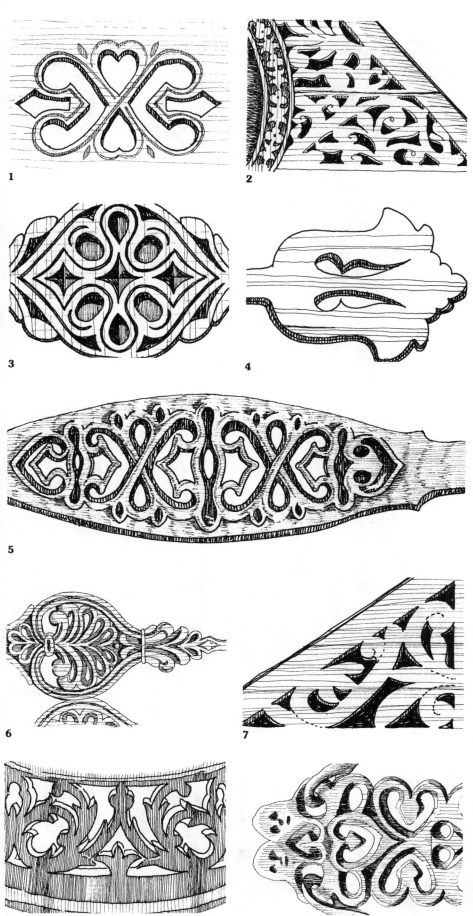

1. Norway—love spoon handle motif; pierced and fretted, knife-carved (nineteenth century).

2. Romania, Transylvania—gable end of a peasant's house; pierced, fretted, and adze-worked (nineteenth century).

3. Scandinavia—domestic spoon motif; chip-carved with a knife (nineteenth century).

4. Romania, Transylvania—gable of a peasant's cottage, detail; pierced, adze-carved, and sawn (nineteenth century).

5. Norway—love spoon handle; fretted and knife-carved in pine (nineteenth century).

6. Norway—engagement spoon, detail; fretted and knife-carved (nineteenth century).

7. Romania, Transylvania—cottage gable decoration; sawn and fretted (nineteenth century).

8. England—Chippendale coaster; fretted and carved, sawn and chiselled (eighteenth century).

9. Norway—love token spoon handle with carved wooden "chain" attachment; pierced and knife-carved (nineteenth century).

129

Art Nouveau

1. France—mahogany exhibition stool carved by Jacques Gribb; built-up and gouge-worked (late nineteenth century).

2. Germany—cabinet, detail; laminated in flat plywood and carved (late nineteenth century).

3. Germany—table bracket, detail; fretted and sawn in laminated wood (late nineteenth century).

4. United States—teak bench back carved by Charles Green; built-up, sawn, gouge-carved, and incised (twentieth century).

5. Italy—window above a door; built-up, carved, and incised (nineteenth century).

6 and 7. Europe—chair back, detail, by Charles Rohlfs; built-up, sawn, fretted, gouge-carved, and incised (nineteenth century).

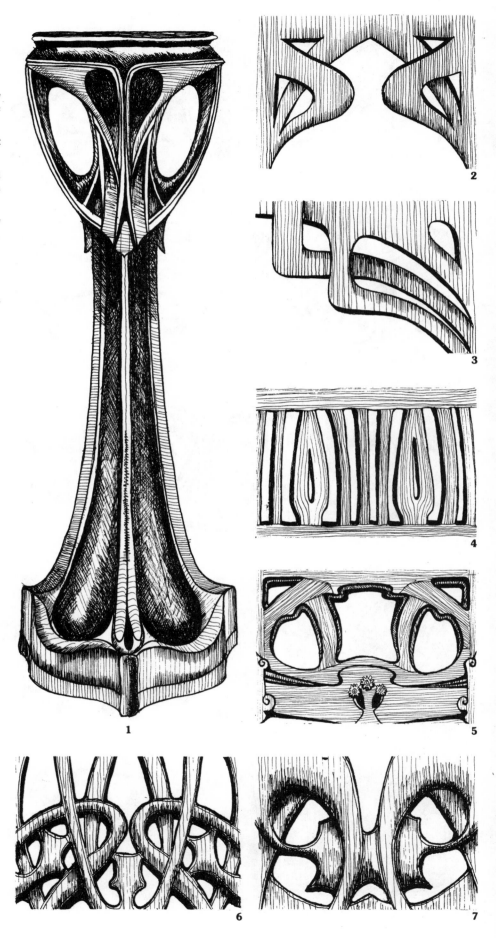

1

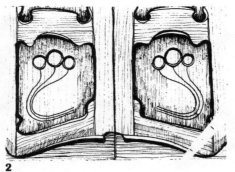

2

4

3

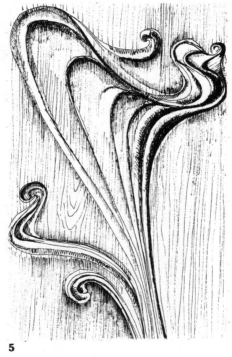

5

6

7

1. Spain—furniture panel, detail; relief-carved, the ground cut away and punched (1900).

2. Italy—door panel; built-up, carved, and incised (1900).

3. Germany—door panel; joined, built-up, and carved, worked with carpenter's tools and gouges (1900).

4. Italy—door panel, door surround, and window above the door; built-up, carved, and incised (1900).

5. Denmark, Copenhagen—wardrobe, detail; deeply gouge-carved and incised (1900).

6. France—sewing table stretcher; built-up, pierced, chip-carved, and incised (twentieth century).

7. France—cupboard, detail; built-up, jointed, and gouge-carved (1900).

1. England(?)—oak chest carved by G. Washington Jack; built-up, jointed, relief-carved, and chip-carved (nineteenth century).

2. England—bookcase; built-up, carved, and painted, worked with saws, gouges, chisels, etc. (nineteenth century).

3. France—screen by Emile Galle; built-up, glued, carved, painted, and incised (1900).

1

2

1. Dutch East Indies—cabinet panel; built-up and gouge-carved, worked in a fine hard wood (seventeenth century).

2. Mexico (Spanish)—set of measures; knife-carved in low relief (eighteenth century).

133

Furniture Inlay and Marquetry

1. England—William Morris table, marquetry motif; cut and worked in three types of wood (nineteenth century).

2. Spain—chest; thick inlay, worked in at least three different types of wood (sixteenth century).

3. Spain—chest, inlaid motif; cut to a depth of about 1/4″ and worked in two types of wood (sixteenth century).

4. Spain—inlaid Varguenos chest; worked in painted, tinted, and scorched woods (sixteenth century).

5. England—sideboard panel, detail, a marquetry design; cut and worked in two thin veneers (nineteenth century).

6. England—commode motif; inlaid in two types of wood (eighteenth century).

7. Spain, Catelonia—chest; deeply cut inlay worked in a single wood (sixteenth century).

8. Spain—furniture design; thickly cut marquetry, worked with two wood types (sixteenth century).

9. England—"Gothic" Pugin table, marquetry design; worked in thin woods and painted (sixteenth century).

10. England—tester bed frieze, detail; worked in boxwood and holly (sixteenth century).

1

2

3

4

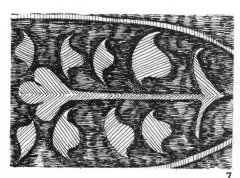
5

6

7

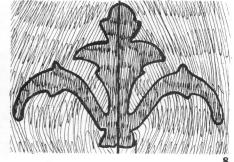
8

9

10

1. Netherlands—Dutch cabinet; worked in marquetry (seventeenth century).

2. England—commode design; worked in marquetry with veneers that are tinted, scorched, and painted (eighteenth century).

3. Denmark—commode motif; inlay, worked in two woods (nineteenth century).

4. Germany—bureau; veneer-worked marquetry (nineteenth century).

5. England—"Gothic" furniture motif, marquetry design; worked in thin veneers and painted (nineteenth century).

6. England—harewood box; worked in scorched and tinted sycamore (seventeenth century).

7. Italy—cabinet design; inlaid and banded using two types of wood (eighteenth century).

8. England—table design; cut and fitted with two wood types (nineteenth century).

9. England—commode door motif; worked in brightly painted and tinted veneers (eighteenth century).

10. France—cabinet motif; deeply inlaid in several wood types (sixteenth century).

Flower Heads

1. Dutch East Indies—cabinet motif; gouge-cut in shallow relief and incised (seventeenth century).

2. India—gable end motif; chip-carved, worked with a knife (sixteenth century).

3. Dutch East Indies—motif from a cupboard door; gouge-cut in shallow relief and knife-incised (seventeenth century).

4. Burma—teak doors; deeply carved and undercut, worked with adze and gouge (seventeenth century).

5. Dutch East Indies—cabinet motif; worked in shallow relief, very fine-grained, knot-free wood (seventeenth century).

6. Mexico (Spanish)—domestic measuring bowl; knife-carved in shallow relief and then incised (eighteenth century).

7. Dutch East Indies—cabinet; carved in shallow relief and knife-incised (seventeenth century).

8. Mexico (Spanish)—food bowl motif; shallowly carved and incised (eighteenth century).

9. Dutch East Indies—cupboard design; knife-worked in shallow relief (seventeenth century).

10. Mexico (Spanish)—bowl pattern; knife-worked in shallow relief (nineteenth century)

1

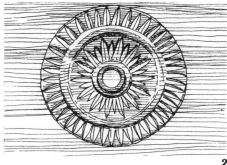

2

3

4

5

6

7

8

9

10

136

1

2

3

4

5

6

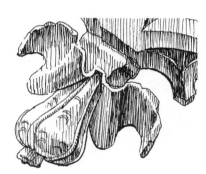

7

8

9

10

1. England—Jacobean(?) four-poster bed design, strap-work motif; carved in shallow relief, gouge and knife work (seventeenth century).

2. England—picture frame by Grinling Gibbons, detail; three-dimensionally worked in lime wood, gouge-carved (seventeenth century).

3. England—Jacobean(?) oak wall panel; flat-worked, shallow-carved (seventeenth century).

4. England—chest motif; gouge-carved rose motif by G. Washington Jack (nineteenth century).

5. England—medieval oak wall panel design; flat-carved with the ground cut away (late sixteenth century).

6. England—chest motif by G. Washington Jack; worked in shallow relief (nineteenth century).

7. England—Gothic tracery; pierced and three-dimensionally carved (fifteenth century).

8. France—throne chair motif; carved in shallow relief, painted, and gilded (early nineteenth century).

9. England—Gothic tracery; pierced and three-dimensionally carved (fifteenth century).

10. France—throne chair motif; carved in shallow relief, painted, and gilded (early nineteenth century).

Floral Panels

1. England—Gothic(?) bed, linenfold panel, detail; worked and carved with plough planes and gouges (fifteenth to sixteenth centuries).

2. Spain—chest; carved in shallow relief, chip-carved, and incised (eighteenth century).

3. Spain—cupboard design; carved in shallow relief, worked with knife and gouge (sixteenth century).

4. Germany—chest motif; carved in shallow relief, some incised work (fifteenth century).

5. Spain—cupboard; carved in shallow relief, knife and gouge work (sixteenth century).

6. Spain—box/chest; pierced, backed, and gilded (fifteenth to sixteenth centuries).

7. Germany—chest pattern; carved in shallow relief with most of the ground around the motif cut away (sixteenth century).

8. England—Gothic church panel; deeply gouge-carved and undercut (fifteenth to sixteenth centuries).

9. Germany—chest panel; carved in shallow relief (sixteenth century).

10. Spain—wardrobe; deeply and intricately gouge- and knife-carved (seventeenth century).

1

2

3

4

5

6

7

8

9

10

1. Switzerland—bed panel; flat strap-work, ground cut away, worked with gouge and knife (seventeenth century).

2. Spain—chest; deeply carved and worked with gouge and knife (eighteenth century).

3. Switzerland—cupboard panel; flat-carved strap-work. (eighteenth century).

4. Malaysia—furniture panel; pierced and fretted, worked with saws, drills, and gouges (nineteenth century).

5. Italy—chest panel; ground cut away and filled with colored mastic (fifteenth century).

6. England—Grinling Gibbons organ case; built-up, glued, and pinned, gouge-worked in lime (seventeenth century).

7. Germany—cupboard panel; flat-carved strap-work, gouge and chisel (sixteenth century).

8. England—Grinling Gibbons organ case; built-up, glued, and pinned, gouge-worked in lime.

9. Malaysia—panel, hibiscus motif; knife- and gouge-carved (nineteenth century).

10. Spain—Renaissance church choir stalls; deeply gouge-carved.

European Leaves and Petals

1. England—credence or sideboard; chip-carved with gouge (fifteenth century).

2. England—dollhouse furniture; gouge-worked chip-carving (eighteenth century).

3. Netherlands—Dutch salad chopper motif; carved in shallow relief and gouge-worked (early eighteenth century).

4. Spain—chest motif, gouge-carved in shallow relief (eighteenth century).

5. England—snuff rasp decoration; chip-carved with gouge, punch-textured ground (eighteenth century).

6. Germany—table motif; relief-carved and gilded (eighteenth century).

7. England—tea caddy motif; carved, gilded, and pinned to a veneered ground (eighteenth century).

8. England—furniture panel motif; carved in deep relief on a painted ground (seventeenth century).

9. England—wall panel; built-up, glued, pinned, and carved, worked with gouge and chisel (seventeenth century).

1

2

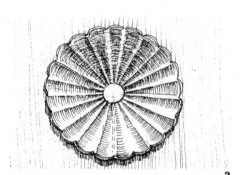

3

4

5

6

7

8

9

1

2 **3**

4

5

1. Norway—chest motif; jointed and carved in shallow relief (eighteenth century).

2. England—bookcase panel; built-up and gouge-carved (eighteenth century).

3. England—spice cup; incised design, worked with a knife (early seventeenth century).

4. Switzerland—chest panel; deeply worked with drill, gouge, and chisel (seventeenth century).

5. England—church ceiling boss or stud; deep gouge work, drilled (fifteenth century).

1. France or Italy—throne chair, possibly made by George Jacob; built-up, gouge-carved, painted, and gilded (early nineteenth century).

2. France—pedal harp; built-up, turned, deeply gouge-carved, and gilded (eighteenth century).

Grand Gilding

1. England—mirror frame; built-up, glued, pinned, carved, pierced, and gilded; worked with planes, gouges, and chisels (eighteenth century).

1

Grand Gilded Mounts

1. England—side table, detail; gouge-carved and applied to a polished ground (eighteenth century).

2. England—mirror frame mount; built-up, glued, and pinned, carved and gilded (eighteenth century).

3. England—mirror frame; built-up, glued, pinned, gouge-carved, and gilded (eighteenth century).

4. England—mirror frame base; built-up, pinned, gouge-worked, and gilded (eighteenth century).

5. England—pine mirror mount; built-up, pinned, carved, and gilded, worked with drill and gouge (early nineteenth century).

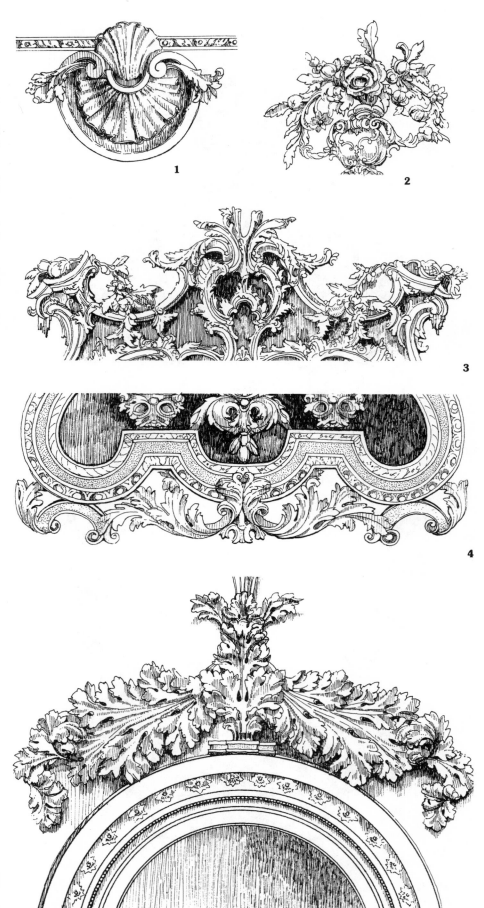

1

2

3

1. Germany—buffet mount; built-up drilled, pierced, gouge-carved, and polished (seventeenth century).

2. England—cabinet mount; built-up, massively gouge-carved, and silvered (seventeenth century).

3. England—cabinet mount; deeply gouge-carved, pierced, and silvered (seventeenth century).

4. France—side table hanging mount; built-up, pierced, gouge-carved, and gilded (seventeenth century).

4

145

Grinling Gibbons and Others

1. England, Berkshire, Windsor Castle—picture frame by Grinling Gibbons, now in the King's Eating Room; built-up, pinned, and gouge-carved (seventeenth century).

2. England, Berkshire, Windsor Castle—over-mantel in the Queen's Presence Chamber; built-up, pierced, and carved in lime wood (seventeenth century).

3. England, London, Mercer's Hall—wall panel, in the style of Grinling Gibbons; built-up, pinned, glued, pierced, and carved (seventeenth century).

4. England, Lincolnshire, Belton House—chapel carving by Edmund Carpenter; carved and mounted, worked with gouge and chisel (seventeenth century).

5. England—the Cosimo Panel, detail, by Grinling Gibbons (now in Bargello Museum, Florence); built-up and gouge-carved (seventeenth century).

6. England, London, St. Paul's Cathedral—panel, detail, by Grinling Gibbons; built-up, carved, and mounted (seventeenth century).

7. England—the Cosimo Panel, detail; built-up, pierced, and gouge-carved (seventeenth century).

1

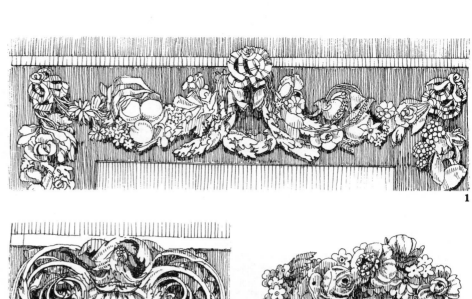

2

3

4

5

6

7

1. England—chest; deep relief gouge work; the design was taken from Verrocchio's tomb of the Medici, 1472, Florence (eighteenth century).

2. England—candle stand base, detail; built-up, fretted, and gouge-carved (eighteenth century).

3. Italy—chestnut chair; built-up, pierced, gouge-carved, and painted; worked with saw, adze, and gouge (sixteenth century).

147

1. England—mirror frame by Grinling Gibbons; built-up and gouge-carved (seventeenth century).

2. England, Lincolnshire, Belton House—wall panel, detail, by Edmund Carpenter; built-up and gouge-carved (seventeenth century).

3. England, Lincolnshire, Belton House—three-dimensional wall panel, detail; built-up and gouge-carved flowers and peas (seventeenth century).

1

2

3

Grinling Gibbons

1. England, Sussex, Petworth House—wall panel, detail; built-up and gouge-carved (seventeenth century).

2. England, Berkshire, Windsor Castle—overmantel, detail, by Grinling Gibbons; built-up, pierced, and gouge-carved (seventeenth century).

3. England—the Cosimo Panel, detail, by Grinling Gibbons; built-up and gouge-worked in lime wood; considered to be Gibbons' masterpiece (seventeenth century).

4. England, Berkshire, Windsor Castle—panel, detail, by Grinling Gibbons (seventeenth century).

5. England—panel, detail, by Grinling Gibbons (seventeenth century).

1. England, Nottingham—medieval(?) panel from a private house; low relief gouge-work, punch-textured ground.

2. England—two halves of a butter mold; deep-cut gouge and chisel work (eighteenth to nineteenth centuries).

3. Italy—pillar; gouge, adze, and knife work (twelfth century).

4. England—Gothic tracery; sawn, pierced, and gouge-carved (fifteenth century).

1

2

3

4

1. England, Leicestershire, Quenby Hall—chest, detail; gouge-carved in flat relief (seventeenth century).

2. England, Leicestershire, Quenby Hall—wall panel; gouge-carved in low relief (seventeenth century).

3. England, Leicestershire, Quenby Hall—four-poster bed, detail; flat-carved strap-work with a shallow cut-away ground (seventeenth century).

4. England, Leicestershire, Quenby Hall—post from a buffet, detail; built-up, turned, and gouge-carved (seventeenth century).

Chapter 5

Animal Forms

African Eyes

1. Liberia (Grebo)—dance mask; knife-worked and pierced (nineteenth century).

2. Mali (Bobo)—dance mask; flat-worked, incised, and painted, adze and knife work (nineteenth century).

3. Mali (Dogon)—black monkey dance mask; hollowed-out trunk wood, cut with adze and knife (nineteenth century).

4. Congo River Area (Bantu)—dance mask; adze-carved, knife-incised, and painted (nineteenth century).

5. Upper Volta (Dogon)—monkey mask; hollowed-trunk wood, adze- and knife-cut (nineteenth century).

6. Upper Volta (Mossi)—mask worn at dances, funerals, and planting ceremonies; flat relief carving, adze and knife work (nineteenth century).

7. Congo River Area (Wabembe)—dance mask; adze- and gouge-worked, painted (nineteenth century).

8. Nigeria (Ogoni)—mask worn at planting and crop-gathering festivals; adze- and knife-worked, and burnished (nineteenth century).

9. Upper Volta (Mossi)—dance mask worn at funerals and ritual harvest or fertility feasts; adze and knife work (nineteenth century).

10. Congo River Area (Bawalwa)—dance mask worn at circumcision rituals; adze and knife work (nineteenth century).

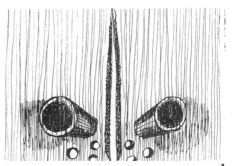
1

2

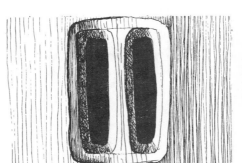
1

2

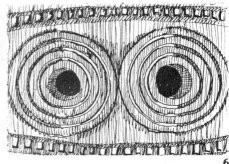
3

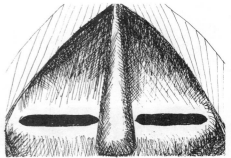
4

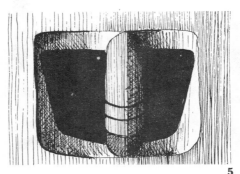
5

6

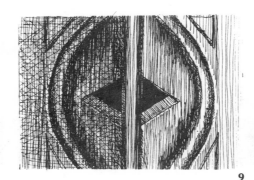
7

8

9

10

1

2

3

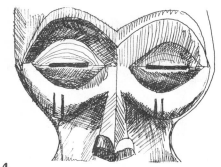

4

5

6

7

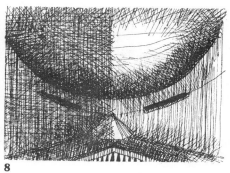

8

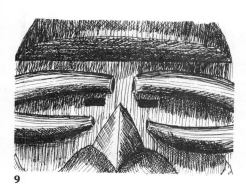

9

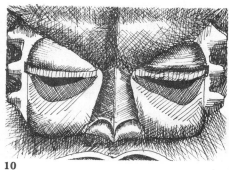

10

1. Nigeria (Ibibio)—secret society mask or yaws skull mask; adze and knife work (nineteenth century).

2. Congo River Area (Batetela)—dance mask; adze-carved and knife-striated (nineteenth century).

3. Congo River Area (Bantu)—heart-shaped mask; adze- and knife-worked, painted (nineteenth century).

4. Congo River Area (Bajokwe)—male "beast" mask to be worn at initiation rites; adze-carved and knife-incised (nineteenth century).

5. Ivory Coast—antelope mask worn for the "leaping" dance; built-up and carved with adze and knife (nineteenth century).

6. Ivory Coast (Baule)—ritual mask; adze- and knife-worked, polished, and burnished (nineteenth century).

7. Nigeria (Wobe)—dance mask; adze, knife, and drill work (nineteenth century).

8. Congo River Area (Bena Kanioka)—sphere mask; adze- and knife-carved, polished, and burnished (nineteenth century).

9. Liberia (Dan)—horned warthog mask; built-up, adze-carved, and burnished (nineteenth century).

10. Nigeria—society mask worn when enforcing the law; adze and knife work (nineteenth century).

155

Tribal Eyes

1. Congo River Area (Basongye)—mask to be worn by a sick person needing spiritual help; adze-carved, knife-striated, and painted (nineteenth century).

2. Ivory Coast Area (Senufo)—dance mask; adze and knife work (nineteenth century).

3. Mali (Bobo)—ritual mask; simple adze work (nineteenth century).

4. Ivory Coast (Senufo)—ancestor dance mask; delicate knife work, polished and burnished (nineteenth century).

5. Ivory Coast (Dan)—animalistic dance mask; roughly finished adze and knife work (nineteenth century).

6. Ivory Coast (Baule)—Gu society mask; highly polished finish, decorated with brass studs, adze and knife work (nineteenth century).

7. Africa—heart-shaped dance mask; carved and painted, adze and knife work (nineteenth century).

8. Mali (Dogon)—mask worn at funeral ceremonies; roughly finished adze work (nineteenth century).

9. Mali (Dogon)—white monkey mask; very basic pierced block with applied hair fringe (nineteenth century).

10. Ivory Coast—woman's black panther mask; fine adze and knife work, polished and burnished to a high finish (nineteenth century).

1

2

3

4

5

6

7

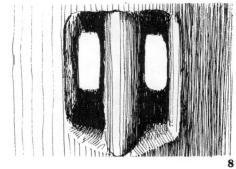

8

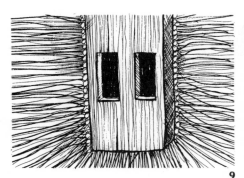

9

10

1

2

3

4

5

6

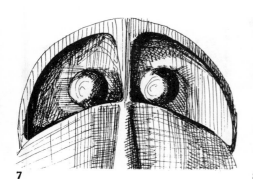

7

8

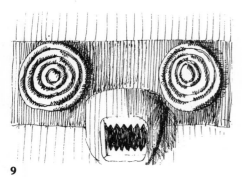

9

10

1. Cameroons (Bamileke)—human face mask, detail; knife-worked and incised, sometimes painted (nineteenth century).

2. Gabon (Fang)—heart-shaped ritual mask; dish-carved, knife-worked, and painted (nineteenth century).

3. Ivory Coast (Dan)—animalistic dance mask; fine adze and knife work, polished and highly burnished finish (nineteenth century).

4. Cameroons (Bafo)—ritual mask; adze-dished, knife-patterned, and painted (nineteenth century).

5. Cameroons—wooden pillar in the royal compound, detail; realistic adze and knife carving (nineteenth century).

6. Congo River Area (Bajokwe)—female "beauty" mask; fine adze and knife carving, high finish, and applied hair (nineteenth century).

7. Ivory Coast (Baule)—dog's head/monkey mask worn at the "soul judging rituals"; deep adze and knife work (nineteenth century).

8. Mali (Bambara)—anthropomorphic mask; roughly adze-carved directly from trunk wood (nineteenth century).

9. Mali (Bobo)—dance mask; flat-carved and built-up adze and knife carving, sometimes painted (nineteenth century).

10. Congo River Area (Bapende)—death mask; adze-carved, painted (nineteenth century).

African Masks

1. Gabon (Fang)—dance mask; knife-carved and smoothly polished (nineteenth century).

2. Nigeria (Ijo)—Otobo water spirit mask; flat-carved and built-up, adze work (nineteenth century).

3. Congo River Area (Basongye)—figure, detail; adze and knife work with nail head scarification patterns (nineteenth century).

4. Congo River Area—Azande figure; three-dimensionally worked, polished and burnished, adze and knife work (nineteenth century).

5. Congo River Area (Bajaka)—drum figure, detail; knife-carved and polished (nineteenth century?).

6. Congo River Area (Bajokwe)—spirit figure, detail; fine knife work (nineteenth century?).

7. Sierra Leone—mask, detail; flat-carved and built-up, adze and knife work (nineteenth century).

8. Africa—Ejiri, or "life force spirit" mask; deeply adze-worked, and textured (nineteenth century).

9. Cameroons (Bamum)—circumcision mask; dish-carved, knife-worked, and painted (nineteenth century).

10. Cameroons (Bafum)—ancestor figure, detail; carved from a hollow trunk, knife-worked, and roughly finished (nineteenth century).

1

2

3

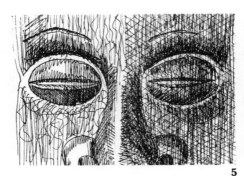

4

5

6

7

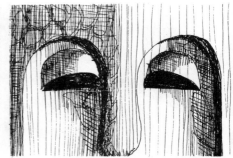

8

9

10

1

2

3

1. Congo River Area (Basongye)—striated mask; adze-carved and knife-patterned, sometimes painted (nineteenth century?).

2. Congo River Area (Bayaka)—puberty mask; carved, built-up, and painted, hair applied (nineteenth century).

3. Ivory Coast (Baule)—society mask; adze and knife work (nineteenth century).

Idols and Masks

1. Congo River Area—dance mask; built-up, adze-carved, and painted; work of this region and character inspired the cubists (nineteenth century).

2. Congo River Area, Kwango River—figure, detail; three-dimensionally carved (nineteenth century?).

3. Nigeria—society mask; built-up, applied, carved, pierced, and painted; adze, knife, and drill (nineteenth century?).

4. Ivory Coast (Baule)—characteristic mask; highly polished finish, adze and knife work (nineteenth century).

5. Upper Volta (Senufo)—ritual figure; axe and knife work (nineteenth century?).

6. Ivory Coast (Guro)—antelope mask, detail; built-up, applied, knife-carved, and painted (nineteenth century?).

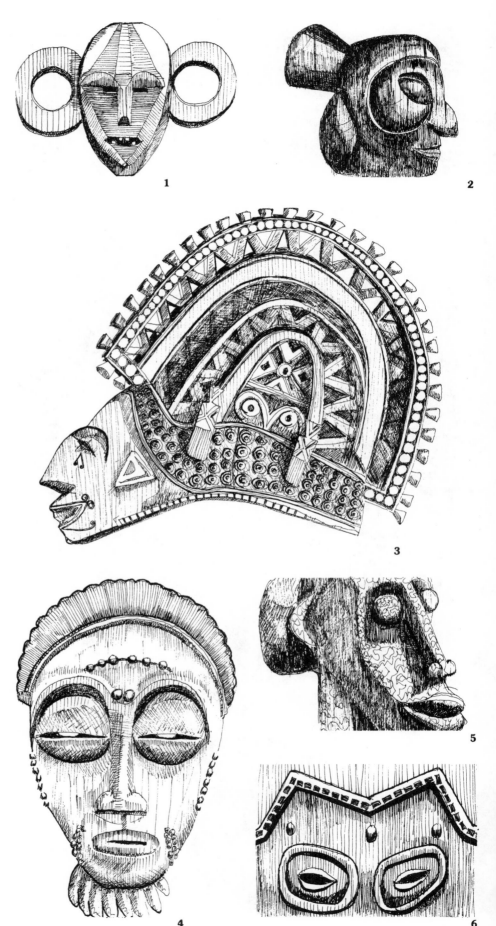

160

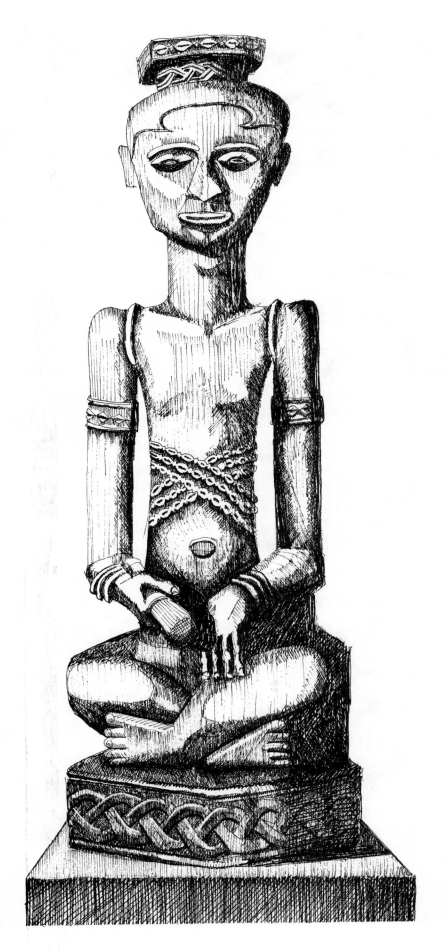

1. Congo River Area (Bakuba)—statue of king Kwete Peshanga; three-dimensionally adze-carved, knife- and gouge-worked; has fine finish and highly polished patina (nineteenth century).

1

161

African Expression

1. Cameroons (Bamileke)—chief's guard mask; knife-carved striations and a fine finish (nineteenth century?).

2. Ghana (Ashanti)—small figure; incised and black-burnished, knife work (nineteenth century?).

3. Congo River Area—ancestor cult figure: fine knife work (nineteenth century).

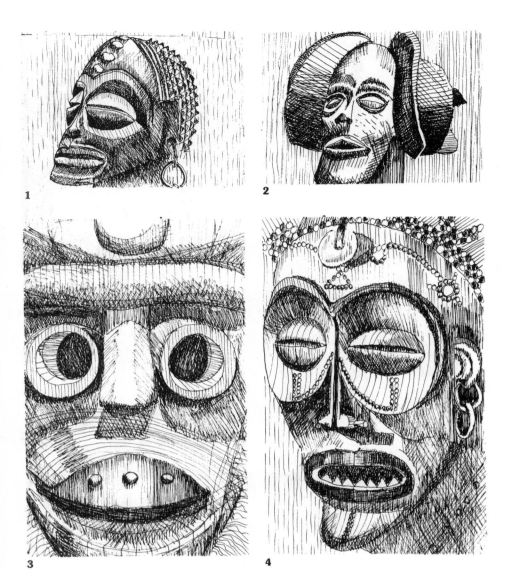

1. Angola—figure detail taken from a chief's stool; very fine knife work (nineteenth century).

2. Angola—female figure head detail, shows characteristic hair style; adze-carved and knife-patterned (nineteenth century?).

3. Nigeria (Ibibio)—thanksgiving mask worn at harvest time; built-up, adze and knife work (nineteenth century).

4. Congo River Area (Bajokwe)—woman's mask with characteristic pointed teeth and "slit plum" eyes; adze and knife work (nineteenth century).

5. Angola—"weeping girl" mask with hair and fiber additions; adze and knife work (nineteenth century).

Oceanian Eyes

1. New Guinea—ancestor figure, detail; very basic stone adze and bone knife carving (nineteenth century).

2. Marquesas—house post figure, three-dimensionally worked statue-like figure; finely adze-carved and knife-detailed (nineteenth century).

3. Cook Islands, Rarotonga—face detail of the god Te Rongo; carved three-dimensionally with stone adze and shell knife(?) (nineteenth century).

4. New Guinea—ancestor image; adze- and knife-carved, painted (nineteenth to twentieth centuries).

5. New Guinea, Geelvink Bay—canoe prow figure; adze- and knife-worked, painted, fiber hair is applied (nineteenth to twentieth centuries).

6. New Zealand (Maori)—house relief, detail; stone adze-carved and knife-incised, shell eyes (nineteenth century).

7. Austral Islands—goddess Raivavae, detail; adze-worked and knife chip-carved (nineteenth century).

1

2

3

4

5

6

7

1. Sierra Leone (Mende)—helmet mask; three-dimensionally adze- and knife-carved, polished and burnished (nineteenth century).

2. Nigeria (Ijo)—charm image; knife-worked (nineteenth century).

Oceanian Expression

1. New Guinea, Sepik District—wooden house plaque; relief-carved, adze- and knife-worked, sometimes painted (nineteenth century).

2. New Guinea—figure; carved in the round, adze, knife, and pierced work (nineteenth century?).

3. New Guinea, Sepik District—mask; deep adze and knife work, polished and burnished (nineteenth century?).

2

1

3

1

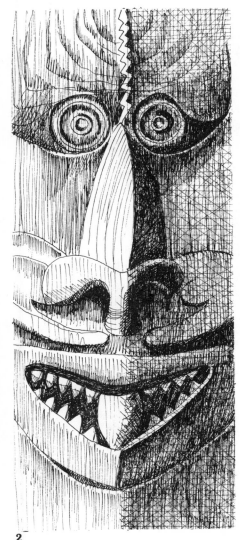

2

3

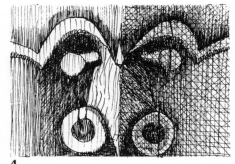

4

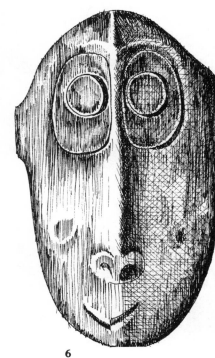

6

5

1. Cook Islands—chief's staff or pole, detail; knife-worked and chip-carved (nineteenth century).

2. New Guinea, Sepik District—gable end, detail; adze-worked and brightly painted (nineteenth century).

3. New Caledonia—roof post, detail; three-dimensionally knife- and adze-worked (nineteenth century?).

4. New Caledonia—roof terminal face; built-up, adze- and knife-worked (nineteenth century).

5. New Hebrides—drum, detail; deeply dish-carved, adze-worked, and chip-carved motifs (nineteenth century).

6. New Guinea, Central Sepik District—ancestor figure face; roughly carved with adze and knife (nineteenth century?).

167

Coastal Totems

1. North America, Northwest Coast—carved club with monster/whale characteristics; carved in the round with a relief-carved surface, adze and knife work (nineteenth century).

2. North America, Northwest Coast (Tsimshian)—mask with characteristic features; knife-carved and shell-decorated (nineteenth century).

3. North America, Northwest Coast—killer whale motif; knife-carved and then motifs lined in with color (nineteenth century).

4. North America, Northwest Coast—stylized mask; painted and carved motifs (nineteenth century).

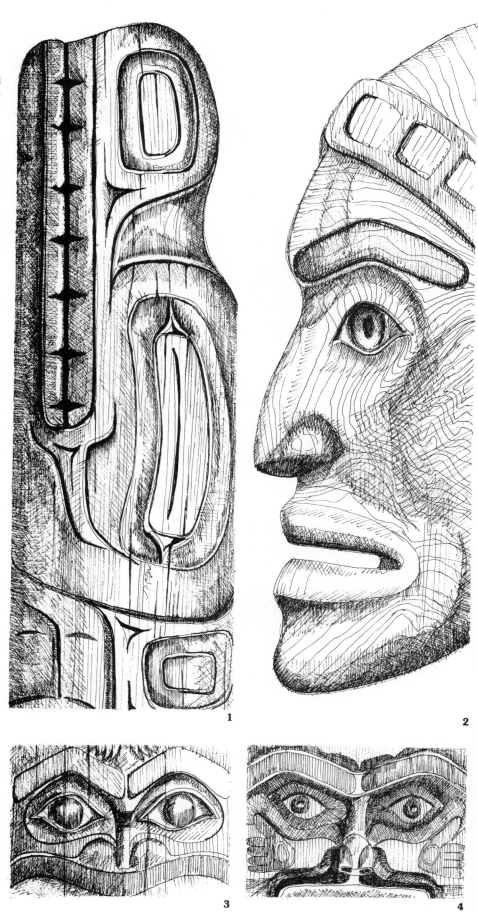

1

2

3

4

168

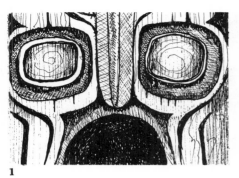

1

2

3

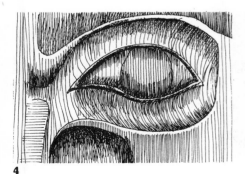

4

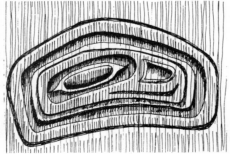

5

1. North America, Northwest Coast, (Tlingit) — sea lion eye and mouth motif; carved in the round with knife and gouge (nineteenth century).

2. North America, Northwest Coast (Tlingit) — nose and eye motifs; carved in deep relief and painted (nineteenth century).

3. North America, Northwest Coast (Salish) — relief carved spindle whorl, worked with characteristic motifs and symbols; knife-carved (nineteenth century).

4. North America, Northwest Coast (Haida) — eye motif from a house post; carved in deep relief (nineteenth century).

5. North America, Northwest Coast (Tlingit) — eye motif from a small box; adze- and knife-carved (nineteenth century?).

Stylized Expression

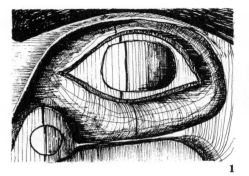

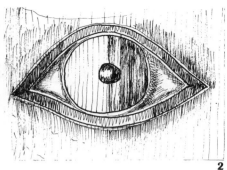

1. North America, Northwest Coast (Tsimshian)—"bear eye" motif; carved in deep relief, knife-worked, and brightly painted (nineteenth century).

2. North America, Northwest Coast (Tsimshian)—eye motif; very shallow, almost incised, work (nineteenth century?).

3. North America, Northwest Coast—house post, detail; carved in the round and surface relief-carved; adze and knife work (nineteenth century?).

1

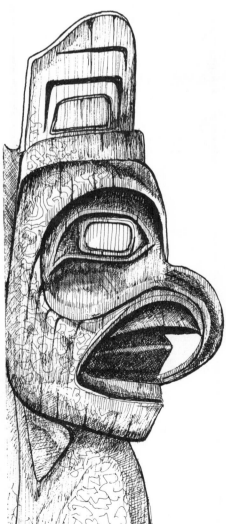

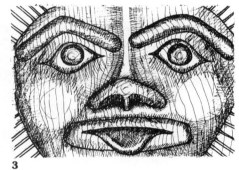

3

4

2

5

1. North America, Northwest Coast—rattle; built-up, knife-carved, and brightly painted (nineteenth century).

2. North America, Northwest Coast—stylized "thunderbird"; deeply carved, painted (nineteenth century).

3. North America, Northwest Coast—cockle shell rattle; built-up, relief-carved, and painted (nineteenth century).

4. North America, Northwest Coast—stylized face, carved and painted (nineteenth century?).

5. North America, Northwest Coast (Tlingit)—dance mask; carved and painted (nineteenth century).

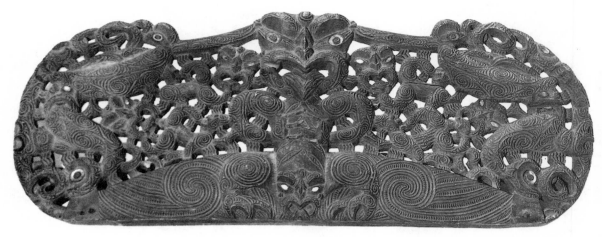

1

1. New Zealand (Maori)—door lintel; relief-carved, pierced, and knife-worked (eighteenth to nineteenth centuries).

2. Cook Islands, Mangaia—ceremonial paddle handle; characteristically chip-carved (nineteenth century).

2

Gods and Images

1. Hawaiian Islands—Ku, the god of war; carved in the round and heavily adze- and knife-worked (nineteenth century).

2. New Zealand (Maori)—house lintel, detail, adze- and knife-worked, pierced, and finely incised (nineteenth century?).

3. New Zealand (Maori)—manaia face, detail; knife-carved, incised, and decorated with shells (eighteenth to nineteenth centuries).

4. New Zealand—house panel; carved in deep relief, complicated incised patterns, decorated with shells (nineteenth century).

1

2

3

4

Maori Images

1. New Zealand (Maori)—door post, detail; carved in deep relief, pierced, and knife-incised (nineteenth century).

2. New Zealand (Maori)—ancestor figure from the wall of a meeting house; deeply carved, pierced, chip-patterned, and incised, shell knife and stone adze used (nineteenth century).

3. New Zealand (Maori)—door lintel, detail; pierced, relief-carved, and incised, adze and knife work (nineteenth century).

4. New Zealand (Maori)—figure detail from a feather box; adze- and knife-carved (eighteenth to nineteenth centuries).

1

2

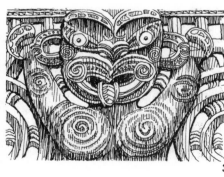

3

4

1

2

3

1. New Zealand (Maori)—beaked animal head; relief-carved and pierced (nineteenth century).

2. New Zealand (Maori)—female figure from a door lintel; pierced, relief-carved, adze and knife work, decorated with shells (eighteenth to nineteenth centuries).

3. New Zealand (Maori)—house panel, detail; relief-carved, pierced, and chip-carved (nineteenth century).

Birds

1. New Guinea—frigate bird and crocodile sculpture from a roof apex; pierced and knife-carved (eighteenth century?).

2. Italy, Sardinia—chest motif incised and chip-carved (seventeenth century).

3. Europe—furniture inlay, crow motif; chisel-cut and worked in a thick dark wood, knife-incised (eighteenth century).

4. Finland—motif from a tankard; three-dimensionally carved and whittled, knife-carved (early nineteenth century).

5. England—Jacobean bench end, peacock motif; deeply carved, gouge-worked, and undercut (seventeenth century).

6. Spain—choir stall panel; carved in deep relief, gouge and adze work (seventeenth century).

7. France—chest panel with fish, bird, and claw motifs; adze and gouge carving (fifteenth century).

8. Netherlands—Dutch warming pan cover; pierced, fretted, and gouge-carved (eighteenth century).

9. France—cabinet, marquetry motif; cut and worked with at least two woods (eighteenth century).

10. England, Lincolnshire, Burghley House—panel carved by Demontreuil; three-dimensionally carved and mounted (eighteenth century?).

1

2

3

4

5

6

7

8

9

10

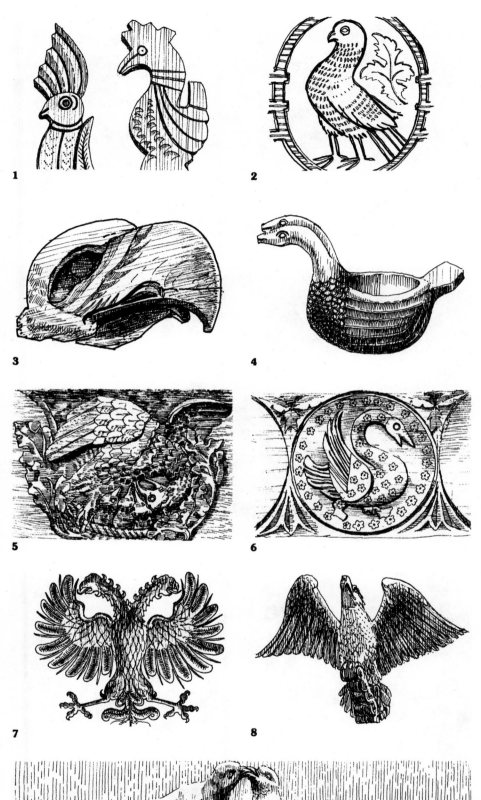

1. Romania, Transylvania—spoon love token; knife carved and incised, sometimes painted (nineteenth century).

2. England—wooden tankard motif; knife-incised and chip-carved (seventeenth century).

3. North America, Northwest Coast (Kwakiutl)—stylized eagle mask; deep, three-dimensional, realistic carving worked with gouge and knife, brightly painted (nineteenth century).

4. Norway—"ale hen" mug; gouge-shaped and knife-decorated (eighteenth century).

5. England—misericord; adze, knife, and gouge carving, deeply undercut (thirteenth century).

6. Germany—chest motif; shallow relief work and chip-carved pattern (fourteenth century).

7. Germany—pastry/cake mold; shallowly dish-carved, worked with knife and gouge (sixteenth century).

8. United States—ship's figurehead; built-up, adze- and gouge-carved, brightly painted and gilded (nineteenth century).

9. England—the Cosimo Panel by Grinling Gibbons, detail; built-up and laminated, worked with shaped and bent gouges (seventeenth century).

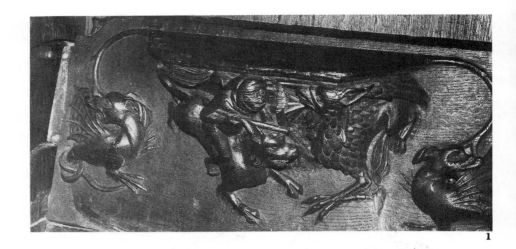

1. England, Newark, Nottinghamshire, St. Mary's—misericord that represents fighting man and eagle; adze- and gouge-carved (sixteenth century).

2. England, Newark, Nottinghamshire, St. Mary's—misericord that illustrates the fable of the owl and the mouse; adze- and gouge-carved (sixteenth century).

3. England, Newark, Nottinghamshire, St. Mary's—bench end that illustrates a carver's joke; adze- and gouge-carved (sixteenth century).

4. England, Newark, Nottinghamshire, St. Mary's—bench end handhold; adze- and gouge-carved (sixteenth century).

Misericords

1

1. Wales, Pembrokeshire, St. David's Cathedral—misericord titled "The Boat Builders"; adze- and gouge-worked (fifteenth century).

2. England, Flintshire, Chester Cathedral—misericord, a detail from the old English tale of the tiger hunter; adze- and gouge-carved (fourteenth century).

3. England, Dorset, Christchurch Priory—misericord that represents a jester; adze- and gouge-carved (fifteenth century).

4. England, Dorset, Christchurch Priory—misericord that represents a laughing man; adze- and gouge-carved (sixteenth century).

5. England, Coventry, Warwickshire, Holy Trinty Church—misericord that represents the green man or Jack-in-the-green; gouge- and adze-carved (fifteenth century).

6. France, Paris, Notre Dame Cathedral—misericord that represents a man's head; carved in shallow relief (sixteenth century).

7. England, Dorset, Christchurch Priory—choir stall detail that illustrates the tale of the tied hounds; shallow, gouge-carved relief work (seventeenth to eighteenth centuries).

2

3

4

5

6

7

Lions, Dragons, and Beasts

1. Egypt—couch, detail; jointed, built-up, adze- and chip-carved, gilded and painted (2000 B.C.).

2. Egypt—stool, detail; realistically carved, adze- and gouge-worked (2000 B.C.).

3. France—folding chair, detail; gouge-carved and applied (sixteenth century).

4. Scandinavia—domestic pot, lid grip; carved in the round and chip-decorated, gouge and knife work (seventeenth to eighteenth centuries?).

5. Germany—chair, detail; knife-carved and applied (seventeenth century).

6. England—misericord supporter, detail; gouge-carved in high relief (fifteenth century).

7. England—card table, detail; knife-carved motif, applied and gilded (mid-eighteenth century).

8. England—tobacco stopper (small tool used for pressing tobacco into a pipe), detail; knife-carved and pierced (seventeenth century).

9. Sweden—ship's figurehead, detail; three-dimensionally adze- and gouge-carved, painted and gilded (seventeenth century).

10. England—shaving outfit of James I, detail; knife-incised (seventeenth century).

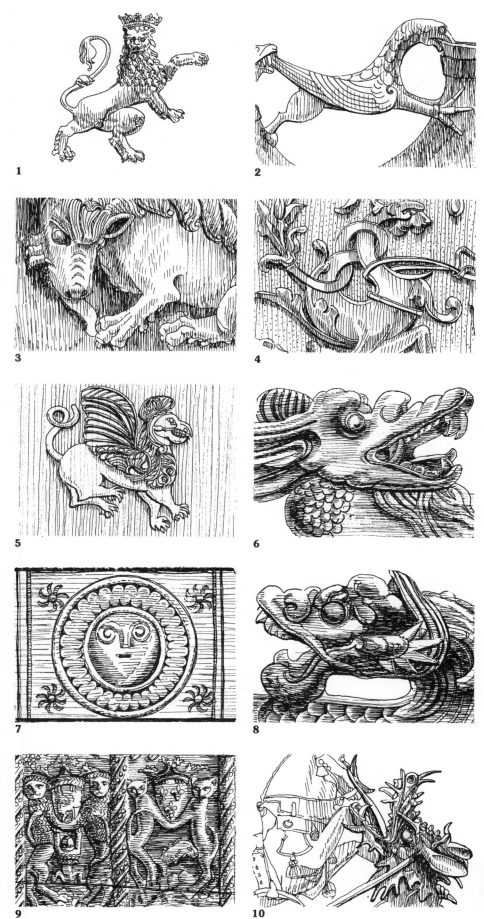

1. England, Cambridge, King's College— gates of a screen, detail; built-up, pierced, and gouge-carved (sixteenth century).

2. Sweden—mug handle; knife-carved and pierced (thirteenth century).

3. England—misericord, detail; deep relief gouge work, pierced and undercut (fifteenth century).

4. Italy—Renaissance cassoni, detail; relief-carved, slightly undercut (fifteenth century?).

5. Norway—wardrobe door panel, detail; carved in shallow relief, incised, and painted (nineteenth century).

6. China—washstand, detail; carved in the round, gouge- and knife-worked, highly polished (eighteenth century?).

7. Italy, Sardinia—chest motif; shallow-carved, incised, and chip-carved (seventeenth to eighteenth centuries).

8. China—washstand, detail; three-dimensionally gouge-carved (eighteenth century?).

9. Netherlands—Dutch chest/box motif; carved in very shallow relief (fifteenth century).

10. Germany—"George and the Dragon" panel, detail; carved in deep relief, pierced and undercut, worked with shaped gouges, painted and gilded (fifteenth century).

181

European Christian Imagery

1. Sweden—Madonna's head, free-standing sculpture; carved in the round, gouge and knife work (twelfth century).

2. Netherlands—"mother and child," free-standing sculpture; carved in the round, deeply worked, undercut and pierced, gouge work (fifteenth century).

3. Spain—"Queen of Heaven," free-standing sculpture; carved in the round, painted, and gilded (thirteenth century).

4. Czechoslovakia, Moravia—"Holy Mother and Child," free-standing sculpture; built-up and gouge-carved, probably painted (early fourteenth century).

5. Germany—"Virgin Mourning," sculpture; realistically worked with knife and gouge (sixteenth century).

6. England—misericord, detail; adze and gouge work in oak (fourteenth century).

7. France—Madonna's head, detail, free-standing sculpture; carved in the round, painted, and gilded (sixteenth century).

8. Germany—"Madonna and Child," sculpture; built-up, worked in the round, gilded, and painted (sixteenth century).

1

2

3

4

6

5

7

8

1. France, Lavandieu—"Christ as King," sculpture; gouge-worked, pierced, and incised (twelfth century).

2. Spain—"John the Baptist," panel; carved in high relief, painted, and gilded (seventeenth century).

3. Flanders—"Jesus Carrying the Cross," built-up panel; carved in high relief, deeply undercut, painted and gilded (sixteenth century).

4. Norway—"St. John," free-standing sculpture; carved and painted (twelfth century).

5. Germany—low relief panel; gouge-worked and undercut, polished (sixteenth century).

6. Germany, Munich—"Christ Crucified," free-standing sculpture; carved and built-up, gouge and knife work (eleventh to twelfth centuries).

7. Germany—choir stall, detail; realistically carved in the round, gouge and adze work (mid-fifteenth century).

8. Germany, Bavaria—"St. George," sculpture; carved and worked in the round, gouge and knife work (fourteenth century).

1

2

4

3

5

1. England, Lincolnshire, Lincoln Cathedral—choir stall; three-dimensionally gouge-worked (late fourteenth century).

2. Netherlands—Dutch(?) oak panel; gouge-carved (seventeenth century).

3. England—mahogany buffet; built-up and three-dimensionally gouge-worked (early seventeenth century).

4. England—oak lectern; built from bits of old carving, gouge-worked (seventeenth century?).

5. England—walnut chair top, detail; gouge-carved (seventeenth century).

184

1

2

Cherubs and Angels

1. England—misericord, characteristic "winged cherub's head"; adze and gouge work (fourteenth century).

2. Italy—mirror frame; built-up and deeply undercarved, gilded (seventeenth century).

3. France—buffet, detail, shallow relief panel; built-up and gouge-worked (sixteenth century).

4. Italy—console table, detail; built-up, jointed, gouge-carved, and pierced (seventeenth to eighteenth centuries).

5. England, Lincolnshire, Belton House—wall panel, probably carved by Edmund Carpenter; built-up and gouge-carved, deeply undercarved (seventeenth century?).

6. Italy—side table, detail; carved in the round, pierced, and gilded (seventeenth century).

7. Italy—cassoni, detail; deep undercut relief work, gouge-carved (sixteenth century).

8. France—side table; three-dimensionally gouge-carved, gilded (seventeenth century).

9. France—wall panel; relief-carved, gouge-worked (mid-eighteenth century).

3

4

5

6

7

9

8

1. Japan—cupboard mount; gouge-carved, pierced, and polished (eighteenth century).

2. Scandinavia—box; deep relief knife- and gouge-worked, and chip-carved (eighteenth century).

3. France—cabinet, detail; three-dimensionally gouge-carved and gilded (nineteenth century).

4. Denmark?—chief's throne; massive construction, adze and gouge work (twelfth century?).

1

2

3

1. Tibet—scripture book cover; carved in deep relief in pine, some chip-carved pattern (eighteenth century).

2. England, Lincolnshire, Belton House—wall panel, detail; built-up, pierced, and gouge-carved (seventeenth century).

3. England, Lincolnshire, Belton House—"Hanging Ducks" panel, detail, carved by Edmund Carpenter; built-up, pierced, and gouge-carved (seventeenth century).

Tools Glossary

ADZE A wood cutting tool that has an arched blade at right angles to the handle, the adze has been used from the earliest times until the present day. This tool in use is swung like a pendulum. Many primitive and ethnic carvers used adzes that had stone and shell cutting heads.

AXE This instrument for cutting or chopping has a heavy head with a cutting edge and is made of steel; in the past the heads have been made of shell, jade, and nephrite. It is used to cut away large areas.

BENCH SCREW This wood holdfast is passed through a hole in the bench surface and then screwed into the base of the wood that is to be worked. It has the advantage over other wood holding devices in that it does not damage the carved surface, nor does it get in the way when the carver is working.

BRACE AND BIT This wood boring tool has interchangeable drill bits and a ratchet movement that enables the user to reverse the handle without withdrawing the bit, making the drilling movement continuous rather than intermittent.

CHISEL This is an edged tool for making straight cuts. In use the shaft is held in one hand and the wooden handle is pushed with the other. For large work the chisel can be held with one hand, while the wooden handle is struck with a mallet.

CLAMP OR CRAMP Known by various patent names, this wood holdfast is usually referred to as a "C" clamp. The screw of the clamp is turned and the wood to be worked is held securely.

COMPASS The compass is an instrument with two legs joined at the top by a pivot. The spike is positioned at the center of the circle required, then a pencil scribes the circle.

DIVIDERS These are used for transferring measurements. The distance between the two hinged legs can be fixed by means of a screw.

DRAWKNIFE The blade of the drawknife has handles at right angles to the cutting edge. In use the tool is gripped in both hands and drawn along the wood. For certain specialized work the blades are sometimes convex or concave.

GOUGE The most important tool of the carver, the gouge is basically a chisel with a concave blade used to cut holes and grooves. There are many gouge types, each designed for a specific task.

KNIFE The carver's knife is an individual tool, and many carvers are quite content to use an old kitchen knife. The main requirement of a good woodcarving knife is that the blade be short and sharp.

MALLET In ethnic societies the mallet is often just a heavy, unshaped piece of wood. For a tool with a longer life, a heavy block of wood is mounted on a short handle so that, in use, the end-grain strikes a chisel or other tool.

PLANE A tool for smoothing, dressing, and cutting boards and planks, the plane comes in many shapes, sizes, and designs. In use it is held and guided in one hand and pushed along the surface of the wood with the other.

PLOUGH PLANE Very much like a plane in design and action, this tool cuts channels, grooves, and moldings. Old plough planes are each designed to cut a specific pattern, but there are now many multipurpose tools on the market.

RASP This hand-held shaping tool comes in all manner of designs, but basically rasps are toothed planes or files. Their main use is cleaning up the surface of the work prior to finishing.

RIFFLER This small, spoon-shaped file is used for roughing out hollows and difficult corners. Rifflers come in many designs, each of which relates to a specific woodcarving problem.

SAW, COPING Swivel-bladed saws of this type are used for cutting or fretting out intricate patterns in thin sheets of wood.

SAW, TENON OR BACKED Short-bladed saws of this type are used where it is important to have small, precise cuts—joints, roughing out patterns, channel cuts, etc.

STONES AND SLIPS These are for sharpening chisels and gouges. In use the stone is oiled, and either the tool is held and rubbed on the stone or the curves of the cutting tool are stroked with the slip.

VISE This two-jawed, bench-mounted clamp is an essential piece of woodcarving equipment. As with most woodcarving tools and equipment, there are many makes, models, and designs.

General Glossary

ABSTRACT PATTERN These are carved patterns that have evolved from naturalistic plant forms until the original source is obscured.

ACANTHUS This is a conventional ornament resembling the foliage of the acanthus plant. It is also a type of Greek capital design.

ALDER A reddish hardwood that carves well, alder wood lasts for a long time in damp conditions, and is used for posts, chair legs, and clogs.

AMBOYNA A hardwood that comes from the Andaman Islands, it has beautiful patterns when polished. In timber form it was once used by the European furniture makers, but now it is sold mainly in thin veneers.

ANIMAL DESIGNS These are carved forms and motifs that derive their shape from animals, e.g., ball and claw or lion chair legs.

APPLE A close-grained hardwood, apple wood was once used mainly for small bowls or dishes; it turns and carves well.

BALL AND TONGUE This is a carving term that refers to pattern of molding that looks rather like alternating eggs and bird tongues. This motif became popular in English and European seventeenth-century grand house interiors.

BALSA The lightest known wood (about half the weight of cork), balsa comes from the West Indies and South America. Although it is classified as a hardwood, it cuts easily and is good for use in simple model carving.

BAROQUE CARVING As a generalization this term is used to describe the period from the seventeenth to the eighteenth centuries when art and architecture in Europe moved toward dramatic and vivid forms.

BEECH A European hardwood that cuts, carves, and turns well, it is mainly used for bentwood furniture, tool handles, and toys. Although it is light in color and smooth in texture, it is difficult to polish.

BENCH, CARVER'S This is a solid table used by carvers and woodworkers; although it is usually specially built, any good stout table can be used. It is usually fitted with a gripping device.

BLEMISHES These are faults, such as cavities, knots, or splits, in the wood that can interrupt or spoil the work.

BIRCH The best types of this hardwood are Canadian and American. Birch carves and works well and is used for kitchen ware and simple furniture.

BOW DRILL This is a wood boring tool that is powered by a small bow and a stone or metal weight. In use the shaft of the drill is supported with one hand, and the bow is pushed backwards and forwards; the weight supplies the momentum.

BOXWOOD This hardwood is smooth-textured and fine-grained and the best varieties come from Europe and Asia. It carves well, takes a good polish, and gives off a pleasant scent when cut. Boxwood is used for all manner of small carved work.

BRASS STUD WORK In this technique, which is much used in North African carving, the wood is carved and patterned and then the main motifs are outlined by the heads of small brass nails.

BUILT-UP CARVING In this technique the basic shape is roughed out in glued and jointed blocks of wood prior to carving. It is used primarily by European carvers when carving statuary that has projections such as arms or legs.

BURNISHING To achieve a high finish and polish, oils, waxes, or plant juices are rubbed into the surface of the wood.

CASSONI These Italian Renaissance marriage coffers or dowry chests were richly carved and decorated with motifs, pattern, and family arms.

CEDARWOOD A softwood, cedarwood comes in large sections, is straight-grained, is inexpensive, and works well. It also weathers well and retains tooling, which makes it a good material for use in park and garden sculptures. The best varieties come from California and British Columbia.

CHERRY WOOD A close-grained hardwood, cherry wood carves well and takes a good polish. It is ideal for small pieces of high finish work.

CHESTNUT WOOD This hardwood was much used by Medieval church and cathedral builders. It glues and carves well.

CHIP CARVING In this method of carving relief patterns, small nicks or chips of wood are removed from the surface of the furniture or sculpture with sharp-edge chisels or knives.

CLOSE-GRAINED This refers to wood that has narrow annual rings. Generally speaking a close-grained wood carves well.

COLONNADES This is a series of small, turned pillars or a line of fretted and carved decoration that ornaments a piece of furniture.

CONVOLUTED MOTIFS These spiral or snake-like patterns and motifs are relief-carved in order to give the illusion of knotting or weaving.

CRAFT REVIVAL At the beginning of the twentieth century there was a turn away from industrialized products and a popular demand for art and craft objects that were traditional.

CYPRESS An American hardwood that resists termite attack and decay, cypress carves well and is ideal for such things as boxes and barrels.

DEEP RELIEF CARVING In this technique of carving, figures or motifs appear to project from the wood surface. With deep relief work the carved subjects are undercut so that they are almost three-dimensional.

DOMESTIC CARVINGS These are everyday country articles that can be used in the kitchen or dairy.

DOUGLAS FIR This softwood is sometimes called Columbian pine, Oregon pine, red pine, or yellow fir. It is a firm grained wood that works well, comes in long lengths, and is ideally suited to most mast and spar work. When it is carved, it resists shrinkage and cracking.

DRILL WORK In drill work patterns and motifs are fretted and cut with a saw and drill. Sometimes the drilled holes form the pattern structure.

EBONY This fancy hardwood is very dark in color, commonly purple or black. As it is in short supply, it is usually reserved for small, expensive high finish work.

ELIZABETHAN CARVING This style of carving refers to the period 1558-1603 when Elizabeth I was queen of England. Generally the style is heavily patterned and deeply carved.

ELM This hardwood is heavy-grained and reddish brown in color. It was much used by English carvers in the eighteenth and nineteenth centuries, but its use is now in decline. Elm works well and is best used where strength and resistance to water are vital.

FINISH This is a term used to describe the final texture and appearance of a piece of carving. A piece of wood is said to have a smooth finish, a tooled finish, etc.

FOLIATED CARVING These are carved motifs that relate to plant forms, for example, acanthus or twined vine.

FRET WORK This is a style of carving that is worked on thin sheets of wood. The motifs are cut out in order to form open work, that is to say patterns that reduce the wood to interlaced tracery.

FURROW CARVING In this technique of cutting V-shaped lines in the surface of the wood furrows are made in the surface of the work to form striated pattern.

GILDED CARVING This is carved work that has usually been coated with thin plaster and then thin sheets of gold leaf. For best effect the wood has to be carved in deep relief. In the seventeenth and eighteenth centuries gilded furniture and house interiors were fashionable.

GREEN WOOD This is unseasoned wood that still contains sap; the term usually refers to wood that is worked before it has had time to dry out and season.

GROUND CUTTING This is a method of cutting away the wood so that a motif is left in relief. A coat of arms or a misericord is usually worked so that the ground or background is cut to a lower level.

HARDWOOD This is a close-grained wood from deciduous trees. In practice it doesn't always follow that a hardwood is harder than a softwood, which is from coniferous trees; it is more a term that generalizes the wood's main characteristics.

HAZEL This hardwood is more often called American red gum or Satin walnut. It is a brown yellow in color, close-grained wood that carves,

cuts, and frets well. It is most frequently used for making toys and small pierced and fretted ware.

HEARTWOOD The early growth of the tree, heartwood is usually firm, dark, and full of resins. It has strength but is difficult to work.

HEMLOCK A softwood, this timber usually comes from Canada and the northwest United States. Since this wood is relatively cheap, is pleasant to work, and comes in large widths, it is ideally suited to large interior sculptures.

HICKORY A hardwood from America and Canada, this wood is difficult to work. It is used mainly for tool handles.

HOLLY A fine-grained white hardwood, holly comes only in small sizes and is expensive. For these reasons, it is usually stained and used for small carved work, turning, and decorative inlay.

INLAY This is a technique of cutting holes in the wood surface and letting in pieces of wood of different texture, grain, and color. It is sometimes called intarsia or, depending on the materials used, shell or mastic inlay.

IROKO This African hardwood looks and works very much like teak. It is dark brown in color, close-grained, and polishes well. It is suitable for indoor and outdoor purposes.

INTARSIA *See* Inlay

JACOBEAN CARVING This refers to work from the period of James I of Scotland and England (1566-1625). The carved work of this period was characterized by ribbons and bands carved in flat relief; these are referred to as strapwork.

KNIFE CARVING Many African and Oceanian carvings are worked from the rough timber to completion, the only tool used being a curved knife. American folk knife-carved work is usually referred to as whittled or chipped work.

LAMINATION The term refers to the glueing together of several planks or layers of wood prior to carving.

LARCH A softwood, larch comes from North America, Russia, and Europe. In use this wood is best restricted to simple outdoor sculptures and carvings. It is a difficult wood to work and finish, but it possesses great strength and durability.

LIGNUM VITAE This hardwood comes from South America and the West Indies. A very hard, dense, yellow brown wood, it is used mainly for turning and for small decorative table ware. The best carving mallets usually have lignum vitae heads because in use it resists splitting and bruising.

LIME WOOD This is a hard, close-grained hardwood. Its main quality is that it can be cut in all directions. The seventeenth-century English carver Grinling Gibbons executed most of his work in this wood.

LIME A pigment made from crushed limestone, lime is mixed with gums and used by many tribal carvers in New Guinea and Oceania to inlay masks and shields.

LINENFOLD An English and European panel decoration of the late Gothic period, linenfold is a carved motif representing vertically folded cloth or curtains. It is most commonly found on chests, wall panels, and chair backs.

MAHOGANY Since it comes from many different countries, mahogany is sold as Cuban mahogany, Spanish, Mexican, etc. Each variety has slightly different characteristics, but generally speaking it is red brown in color and is straight, firm-grained, and knot-free. It carves and works well.

MAPLE This hardwood from Canada, the United States, and Europe carves well and takes a beautiful polish, but since it has a fine grain and

pattern, it is used primarily as a decorative veneer.

MARQUETRY This decorative technique differs from inlay in that the sheets of thin veneer are glued to the surface of a base wood. In practice the veneers are cut so that they fit together rather like a puzzle; they are then glued to the base board, sand-finished, and finally polished.

MASTIC This is a tree resin that is used by primitive carvers as a glue or as a base for pigments. Many Oceanian and African carvings are inlaid with a mixture of mastic and white lime; the effect is of crisp, sharp-edged pattern.

MISERICORDS These are bracketed seats that project from the underside of a choir stall. In monasteries, cathedrals, and other Medieval institutions, old monks were granted special permission to rest on the misericords during long services.

MOUNTAIN ASH Known as American ash or Japanese ash, this hardwood has many of the qualities of oak; it is strong, rough-grained, and yellow white in color. Although it works and carves well it sometimes contains unexpected stains and streaks.

OAK This hardwood comes from a great many countries—England, America, Japan among others—and since there are considerable characteristic differences between English oak and American oak, for example, it should be purchased by name of country of origin. Generally the wood is strong and straight-grained but difficult to work.

PATINA In connection with wood, this term refers to the marks, stains, bloom, and oils that wood in long service obtains.

PEAR This beautifully grained hardwood carves and works well and is much used domestically for bowls, spoons, etc.

PIERCED CARVING In this technique wood is fretted, drilled, and cut away so that only a tracery remains.

PINE This is a group name that refers to a great family of woods: Scotch pine, Pitch pine, Yellow pine, to name a few. The main characteristics of this softwood are that it is straight-grained, inexpensive, and pleasant to carve.

RENAISSANCE CARVING This refers to carving that was made sometime between the fourteenth and sixteenth centuries. Renaissance as a term of historical reference differs from country to country, so it is usually necessary to refer to the Italian Renaissance, the German Renaissance, and so forth. Generally a piece of work is said to be Renaissance if it reflects the artistic mood of the period.

REPRESENTATIONAL CARVING This work seeks to copy nature, for example a carved face, a sculpture of a known person, or a carved still life.

ROMANESQUE CARVING This is a general term used for the styles that succeeded the Roman and lasted until the introduction of the Gothic (approximately the eighth to the twelfth centuries).

ROMANTIC CARVING This is carving that expressed Romantic ideas which originated in Germany in the eighteenth century and culminated in an art and crafts movement in England and France in the first half of the nineteenth century.

ROSEWOOD There are several varieties of this hardwood, but the best come from Brazil and the East Indies. Although the wood is attractive to the eye, its variation in density destroys precision tools. It is now used mainly for high grade cabinet work and veneers.

ROUNDEL In woodcarving this term refers to

any motif that is based on a circle. On Medieval boxes and chests there are chip-carved roundels.

SAPELE This hardwood is sometimes known as West African mahogany. In texture and color it is similar to red cedar, and it carves and polishes well.

SOFTWOOD This is wood that comes from coniferous or cone bearing trees. The timber tends to be light in weight, color, and texture.

SPACE FILLERS These are small, not very important side motifs that help to establish the main design.

SPLAT These are the turned and sometimes carved vertical members that fill chair backs.

STEAM BENTWOOD. When wood has been water-saturated and steamed it can be shaped, for example bentwood chairs.

STRAP-WORK This is carved ornamentation in the form of crossed or interlaced bands.

STRIATED PATTERN These are incised or chip-carved lines that decorate a surface. Many primitive African sculptures have striated textures.

SYCAMORE A light-colored hardwood that carves well and is distinctive in that it has no smell or taste, sycamore is used mainly for small kitchen and table ware.

SWAGS These carved motifs that resemble draped cloth were a much used motif on European seventeenth and eighteenth century furniture.

TEAK This hardwood from India and Burma is straight-grained and brown in color. Its oily texture takes a fine polish, but it is difficult to carve.

TUNBRIDGEWARE This is a technique of fine inlay/mosaic that takes its name from Tunbridge Wells in England. This ware is characterized by minute mosaic patterns, scenes, and motifs.

UNDERCUTTING This is a technique of deep relief, almost "in the round" carving. Many English carved church benches have deeply worked motifs that are so undercut that they are only joined to the main body of the work by tenuous "bridges" of wood.

WALNUT A hardwood that is found in most English and European interiors of the sixteenth and seventeenth century, walnut has merit in every aspect: it carves well, takes a beautiful polish, resists shrinkage, and is strong.

Index